365.023

how2become

How to Join the Parachute Regiment

The Insider's Guide

Orders: Please contact How2become Ltd, Suite 2,
50 Churchill Square Business Centre, Kings Hill,
Kent ME19 4YU.

Telephone: (44) 0845 643 1299 - Lines are open Monday to
Friday 9am until 5pm. Fax: (44) 01732 525965. You can also
order via the e mail address info@how2become.co.uk.

ISBN: 978-1-907558-05-4

First published 2010

Copyright © 2010 how2become Ltd.

Typeset for How2become Ltd by Good Golly Design,
Canada, goodgolly.ca

Printed in Great Britain for How2become Ltd by CMP (uk)
Limited, Dorset.

CONTENTS

INTRODUCTION

Dear Sir,

Thank you for purchasing your new guide, How to Join the Parachute Regiment: The Insider's Guide.

As you are probably already aware, Paratroopers are a unique breed of people who are both professional and extremely skilled in everything they do. They have deservedly earned the reputation for being a formidable fighting force and are very well respected by other Armed Forces around the globe.

The Parachute Regiment, known generally as the Paras, is one of the most famous elite regiments of the British Army. The members of the Paras are regarded as some of the most highly trained soldiers in the army. Obviously not everyone can become a Paratrooper, but this guide will give you an idea of what it takes to join one of the world's most prestigious regiments. One thing is for certain - you will have to work harder than you ever imagined and have the determination, grit and courage to succeed. Only the elite few become a Paratrooper.

The selection process for becoming a Para is extremely

tough. There is a very good reason why the Regiment uses the moto "'Utrinque Paratus'. It means 'Ready for Anything'. If you want to be successful during the selection process then you will need to have this motto at the forefront of your mind. Being a Para is about having the right attitude, the right level of professionalism and also the right level of physical and mental fitness.

The purpose of this guide is to prepare you for every element of selection, from interview skills to BARB test through to ADSC preparation. Read the guide carefully and follow the tips that have been provided by the author. During the selection process, focus on the word 'perseverance'. Always look to improve your weaker areas and use an action plan that is focused on improving your abilities. Aim for 100% at all times.

Best wishes,

The how2become team

The How2become team

PREFACE

By Author Richard McMunn

Over the years I have known and worked with a number of ex Paras. I have never met one who was unprofessional, disorganised or unfit. They are, in my opinion, an unbelievable type of person.

The first time I came into contact with a Para was during my career in the Fire Service. I joined Kent Fire Brigade at the age of 21 after serving four years in the Royal Navy. I soon rose quickly through the ranks and at the age of 25 I was a lead instructor on a recruit course, teaching new recruits how to become firefighters. The majority of people who came on the course would struggle to get through the 16 weeks hard basic training. However, I remember on one particular course there was a lad who had just left 1 Para in order to join the Fire Service. As an Officer in the Fire Service I always believed that you should never ask your firefighters to do anything that you wouldn't/couldn't do yourself. So, during the first day of a recruit course, which the ex Para formed a part of, I challenged all 14 new recruits to the bleep test. After level 13 all expect one of them (the ex Para) had

dropped out. It was now down to me and the ex Para to battle it out. You can probably imagine what happened next. I dropped out at level 14; yet he continued up to level 15.6 – very impressive!

Paratroopers are a different breed to your average soldier. They are extremely highly trained. 60% of the soldiers whom form part of the Special Air Service come from 1 Para. So, what does this all mean for you? Well, you don't need to be the finished article when you attend the Parachute Regiment Aptitude Course (PRAC), but you do need to have the right mental attitude and physical fitness. I've designed this guide so that it will give you every chance of success. Keep it by your side whilst you are going through selection and take onboard the tips and advice that are most applicable to your circumstances.

Finally, remember that you are trying to join something extraordinary. Paras are different from your average person. They have a unique state of mind that allows them to achieve anything. Work on your mindset as much as you do your fitness and your chances of success will increase greatly.

Richard McMunn

Richard McMunn

Every effort has been made to ensure that the information contained within this guide is accurate at the time of publication. How2become Ltd are not responsible for anyone failing any part of any selection process as a result of the information contained within this guide. How2become Ltd and their authors cannot accept any responsibility for any errors or omissions within this guide, however caused. No responsibility for loss or damage occasioned by any person acting, or refraining from action, as a result of the material in this publication can be accepted by How2become Ltd.

The information within this guide does not represent the views of any third party service or organisation.

CHAPTER I
THE PARACHUTE REGIMENT STATE OF MIND

The 'state of mind' is the first thing I'm going to help you to develop. Before I even begin to talk about the selection process, the interview or even the PRAC, you must learn how important it is to adopt the correct state of mind. If you have it, then you are far more likely to succeed and pass the selection process for becoming a Paratrooper.

Picture the scene, you are at the PRAC and you are taking part in the assault course. You are totally shattered and your body wants to stop. You've simply had enough and you're not sure that your body can take any more. The majority of other candidates have already stopped and you are desperate to give in. What do you do?

The problem with this kind of scenario is that it is new to you. Not many of us find ourselves in these kinds of situations

ever in our lifetime. Therefore, our minds are not tuned to cope with it and the natural reaction is to quit. Your muscles are telling your mind that they can't take any more and they send a signal to your brain basically saying enough's enough! It's at this point that you're going to be different. This is the difference between your average person and a Para. Regardless of how much you ache, or regardless of how much your body is telling you to quit, your mind will be telling you something completely different. To put it simply, you never give in, even if your body can't move any further along that assault course, you just don't give in.

During my career I've been in this type of situation on numerous occasions. Some of them have been life or death situations. One in particular was whilst serving as a firefighter on White Watch at Maidstone Fire Station. It was approximately 1745 hours on a cold winter's afternoon and I was due to go off shift at 1800 hours. It was a Friday and I was looking forward to going out on the town with my mates. All of a sudden, the bells went down and we were turned out to a fire in a furniture store located in the town centre.

When we arrived, black smoke was billowing out of the front entrance door and windows, and a rather stressful shop owner was urging us to get a move on. As you can imagine, his shop was in serious danger of burning to the ground. I'd not long been out of my recruit training and I had not experienced that many 'severe' fires yet. It was my turn to wear breathing apparatus so I quickly got rigged up, went under air, and then followed the more senior firefighter into the building. What was about to happen was one of the most frightening experiences I have ever encountered in my life. I was about to be tested to the limit.

As we entered the building I could sense something wasn't

quite right. The smoke was becoming thicker and blacker by the second and the temperature was rising quickly. The signs of flashover and backdraught were relatively new to the Fire Service at the time, so we weren't fully aware of the dangerous situation we were entering into. We made our way up to the third floor quickly, taking a hose with us so that we could tackle the fire, and also retrace our steps on the way out. We had been told that the fire was probably in a room on the upper floors of the building, so we started to search for the fire in line with our training and procedures.

After approximately ten minutes the heat inside the building became unbearable, and I couldn't see my hand in front of my face due to the thick, black acrid smoke. I concentrated on my training, took deep breaths and checked my air regularly. I was very fit at the time and hadn't used that much air from my cylinder. My colleague shouted in my ear that he couldn't see the fire anywhere and that maybe we should start thinking about evacuating the building due to the intensity of the heat. I think his words were something more along the lines of "let's get the f#ck out of here, the heat's starting to burn my shoulders!"

Just as we started to retrace our steps we heard a noise that was every firefighter's worst nightmare. Outside, the fire had become so intense that the officer in charge had decided it was time to get us out. Basically, he had initiated the evacuation procedure, which was short blasts of an acme thunderer whistle. All we could hear from inside the building was whistles being blown – we knew we were in trouble. Even though it was a long time ago now, the thought of it still makes the hairs stand up on the back of my neck. I'd heard of incidents where firefighters had lost their lives in fires, and I thought that it might now be my turn.

We quickly started to retrace our steps, following the hose carefully. I'd started to become slightly disorientated due to the heat, but I knew the hose reel would guide us back down the stairs, and to ultimate safety. How wrong could I be! As we approached the top of the stairs the hose suddenly disappeared. My colleague turned to me and shouted that the hose had become trapped under some fallen furniture and he couldn't find the other end of it – we were now in serious trouble. The hose was basically our lifeline, which would lead us to safety, and now we didn't have it. We sat together and took deep breaths. The whistles were still blaring outside and we knew that the only way to get out of this damn building was to try as hard as possible to conserve our air and remain calm. All I could think about was my girlfriend and how much I wanted to see her again. That thought in my mind gave me the confidence and determination to push on and get out of the building to safety.

We decided to locate a wall, and then simply follow it in the direction that our instincts told us would lead to the top of the stairs. We eventually came to the top of some stairs but there was a problem. We could not locate the hose, which effectively meant that this flight of stairs was not the flight we had used to gain access to the building in the first place. Basically we had no choice, we had to go down them and just hope that they led us outside. As we progressed down the stairs my heart was beating like never before. I remember thinking that these stairs could be leading us to a cellar or basement area and that we would become trapped. Thankfully, as we made our way down the stairs we heard voices. The officer in charge had sent in an emergency crew to help locate us. We met them halfway down the stairs and they then led us out to safety. I can remember making my way outside of the building and looking back at the store,

which had already been half demolished by the inferno. Another few minutes in there and I would have been dead, that's for sure. As I took off my breathing apparatus set, which was caked in soot, the officer in charge looked over at me with a huge sign of relief on his face. If only he knew how I was feeling!

I learnt a tremendous amount from that incident. The first thing I learnt was how important it is to remain calm in every crisis situation. Even when things are really bad, the only way that you'll achieve a successful outcome is by staying calm and focused. The second thing I learnt from that experience was the importance of comradeship and teamwork. The Fire Service is very similar to the Parachute Regiment in the fact that everyone looks out for each other. Everyone in the team is dependant on each other. You do your job properly and the team will be just fine. Break the rules, be unprofessional or disorganised, and things will go wrong, it's as simple as that!

Let's take a look at some of the qualities you will need in order to pass selection:

- Confidence

- Strength and physical fitness

- Independence

- Ability

Each one of the above qualities is exceptional in an individual. If you have them all, then you are a serious contender for becoming a Paratrooper. Now I'm not saying that you need to have all of these qualities polished off before you apply to join, but a knowledge of how important they are and also how to demonstrate them in certain situations will go a long way to helping you succeed. Let's now take a look at each of them individually.

Confidence

Confidence is at the top of the list for me personally when it comes to achieving what I want in life. There is a vast difference, however, between confidence and arrogance. I am confident because I believe in my own abilities, I work hard to improve on my weak areas, and I also believe in those people around me. I am not afraid to take risks that I believe are worth taking, and I am certainly not afraid to put my own life at risk to save others. Paras have a confidence about them but they do not feel the need to show off or brag about who they are, or what they are capable of achieving.

Whilst going through selection try to demonstrate confidence, but never cross the line into arrogance. The selection staff want to see that you have the guts to keep running when you're absolutely shattered and when your body is telling you stop. They want to see that that you have the confidence to put yourself forward, when others around you stand back. Confidence comes with time and with experience, but there is no reason why you can't start improving it right now in preparation for selection.

Strength and physical fitness

To the majority of people, the word 'strength' means the ability to lift heavy weights or objects. To the Para, it is not just about physical strength, but also about mental strength. The only obstacle in your way to passing selection is your own mind. Fill it with doubt and negative thoughts and the end result is virtually guaranteed to be failure. Yes, of course you must work on your physical strength and fitness, but if your mind isn't tuned into what you want to achieve, then you are going nowhere, fast!

Allow me to give you an example of where strength of

mind can work to your advantage. Whilst going through the selection process for becoming a firefighter, I was required to attend an intense physical assessment day. Amongst other things, the assessment involved a requirement to:

- Bench press 50kg, 20 times within 60 seconds;

- Run around a field for an hour whilst carrying a heavy object between a small group;

- A claustrophobia test involving crawling through sewer pipes in the dark whilst wearing a blacked out mask;

- Assembling items of equipment;

- Knots and lines;

- Hose running.

The hose running assessment was carried out at the end of the day. Out of twenty people who had started the day, there were just six of us left. Although I was exhausted, there was absolutely no way I was going to fail the hose running assessment. This assessment had a reputation for being gruelling. It entailed running out lengths of heavy hose whilst wearing full firefighting uniform, and then making it back up again in a prescribed manner. It sounds like a simple task, but coupled with the sheer exhaustion that was already taking its toll on my body, and the fact that I was wearing ill-fitting firefighter's uniform, this was no easy task.

The Station Officer started off by making us do ten runs, just to warm up. Whilst we were carrying out the runs, a Sub Officer would walk next to us shouting in our ears how 'useless' he thought we were, and that he knew 'how much we wanted to give in.' After the first ten runs we were then required to do a further 25 more in succession. Soon after we started two men dropped out, leaving just the four

of us remaining. We all managed to complete the 25 runs although I was ready to crumble and I know for certain that I couldn't have done any more. We all stood there in a line with our hoses made up, ready for the next set of instructions. The Station Officer walked up and down with his stick and clipboard, making us wait in anticipation – he was clearly loving every minute of it! My legs were shaking and I could feel my heart pounding so fast it felt like it was about to jump out of my skin.

Then, the Station Officer spoke once more – "OK, pick up your hoses and get ready for another 25 runs!" 25 more runs I thought! You must be joking!

At that point I was at a crossroads in my life. Give in now and all that hard work training to pass firefighter selection would be out of the window. But if I try to press on, then there's absolutely no way I can manage another 25 runs! It was at that point that a thought came into my mind. Whether I could do the next set of 25 runs or not was irrelevant. What was important was that I carried on and I didn't give in. So I did. I picked up my hose and waited for the Station Officer to tell us to commence. He then turned round and said – "Well done guys, you've passed. Put the hoses down and grab yourselves a glass of water." I couldn't believe it; the b#stard was just testing us to see if we had the strength of mind to continue, even though our bodies couldn't take anymore – a valuable lesson in determination and strength of mind if ever I saw one.

Mindset is extremely important whilst preparing for selection. You will need to be organised and disciplined and you will need to concentrate on improving your weak areas.

Independence

The quality of independence is all about being able to look after yourself and being capable of carrying out your role within the team to a professional standard. Once you've completed the rigorous Parachute Regiment training course, you will be expected to look after yourself, your kit and your life in general. Yes there will be continuous training exercises and development sessions, but the overall maintenance of your kit, weapons and physical fitness is down to you. Neglect any of these important elements and you will be letting yourself and the team down.

Paras depend on each other. You will depend on your colleagues within the Regiment to carry out their job to a high standard, and they will depend on you also.

Ability

Ability is the quality of being able to do something, especially the physical and mental power to accomplish something. Not everyone has the ability to become a Paratrooper. These qualities shouldn't be just something that you learn, but they should also be something that you strive to demonstrate during selection. Have the confidence in your own abilities, have the strength of mind to achieve and persevere; be independent and also have the ability to learn new things and accomplish your goals.

TOP TIPS ON HOW TO PREPARE FOR, AND PASS THE PARACHUTE REGIMENT SELECTION PROCESS

TIP I

The right mental approach
Without the correct mental approach your chances of

passing selection will be limited. The majority of people who fail the PRAC do so during the 3.5 mile squadded run at 9min per mile followed by 1.5 mile individual best effort run in 9min 18 to 9min 40 seconds. Even though they are told that they must pass this, many candidates turn up unprepared. This basically means that they don't have the right mental approach. If they can't be arsed to make sure they are capable of running these distances in a certain time, then what chance do they have of passing the training course?

It is vital that you approach your preparation for selection in the right frame of mind. This means getting up early every morning and making sure you can easily pass all of the minimum standards expected during selection. It is also about having the mindset that you will not give in, despite what your body will be telling you. There will be times during selection when you've simply had enough. These are the times when you must push yourself forward and keep going despite the fatigue and the physical agony.

TIP 2

Use an action plan to ensure success

Action plans are a great way to measure your progress during pre-selection preparation. I use an action plan in just about everything I do that is work related. An action plan basically sets out what you intend to do, and when you intend to do it. An example of a very basic action plan that is focused on fitness preparation might look like this:

MONDAY: 6am start, run 3 miles (best effort), and record my time.

TUESDAY: 6am start, 50 press-ups, 50 sit-ups, making sure I concentrate on the correct technique.

WEDNESDAY: 10-mile run, then 50 sit-ups and 50 press-ups, making sure I concentrate on the correct technique.

THURSDAY: Swim 25 lengths of my local swimming pool (breaststroke).

FRIDAY: 6 am start, 10 pull-ups, 50 press-ups and 50 sit-ups, making sure I concentrate on the correct technique.

SATURDAY: Rest day.

SUNDAY: 5-mile brisk walk.

During the next week you may decide to increase the intensity of your workouts and the number of repetitions that you are performing.

The point I am trying to make here is that if you use an action plan, you are far more likely to make significant progress. If you stick the action plan in a prominent position at home, such as the fridge door, then it will act as a reminder of what you need to do the following day.

TIP 3

Don't neglect your aptitude testing ability

Whilst I recommend that you spend the majority of your pre-selection preparation working hard on your fitness, you should not neglect the important area of aptitude testing. During the selection process you will be required to pass the British Recruit Battery (BARB) test. I recommend that you spend at least 30 minutes every evening of the week working on your ability to pass these tests. Within this guide I have provided you with lots of sample test questions to assist you during your preparation. You may also decide to obtain additional online Army BARB testing resources through the website www.how2become.co.uk.

TIP 4

Train hard, race easy

If somebody finds a test or assessment easy, it generally means that they have prepared hard for it. If you work hard in the weeks leading up to the PRAC, then you should find that you pass it with very few problems. Yes, you will find it tough, but if you've trained above the minimum standards that are required, then you will pass with flying colours.

When I was 26 I decided to carry out an Iron Man challenge for a local charity. This involved swimming 2 miles, then running a marathon, before finishing off with a 120-mile cycle ride. I managed to achieve all of this within 9 hours. Whilst it was mentally tough, the physical aspect was easy. It was easy because I'd trained extremely hard in the 6 months leading up to the challenge. Train hard in the build up to selection, and you will certainly race easy!

TIP 5

Bleep test preparation

Lots of people neglect to try out the bleep test before they go through selection. During the selection process you will be required to pass the bleep test, so make sure you can easily achieve this before you go. I recommend being able to achieve level 13. Whilst this is way above the level required, it will stand you in good stead for the PRAC. There are no excuses for not getting yourself a copy of the test and practising it. You can obtain a copy of the test at www.how2become.co.uk.

TIP 6

Technique is crucial

During the PRAC you will be required to carry out as many sit-ups and press-ups as you can within a two-minute period.

Make sure you can do lots of them, but also make sure you use the correct technique. During the build up to selection make sure you practise each of the above utilising the correct technique. This will not only make your life a lot easier during the PRAC, but it will also impress the instructors and show them that you have really gone out of your way to meet their requirements.

TIP 7

You are what you eat (and drink)

Let's face it; a diet of lager, burgers, chips and kebabs isn't going to help you get the most out of your training sessions. In the build up to selection fill yourself with the right types of foods and also make sure you drink plenty of water. You will need the water to keep yourself hydrated.

Foods such as fish, chicken, vegetables, fruit, rice and potatoes are all rich in the right types of nutrients, which will allow you to perform to the best of your ability. Try to cut out caffeine, alcohol and all forms of takeaway food in the build up to selection. You will feel a lot better for it and you will be able to work harder and longer.

TIP 8

Practise a mock interview

Before you attend the AFCO interview, and even the PRAC, try out a mock interview at home. A mock interview basically involves getting a friend or relative to sit down and ask you all of the interview questions that are contained within this guide. This will give you the opportunity to practise your responses to the questions before you do the real thing. The Parachute Regiment selecting officers are looking for people who are confident in their own abilities. During the interview you will want to portray a level of confidence and you can

achieve this by working through your answers before you attend the real thing.

I also recommend that you work on your interview technique. This involves:

- Walking into the interview room looking smart and well presented. Stand tall and do not slouch.

- Don't sit down in the interview chair until invited to do so.

- Be respectful and courteous towards the interview panel. Address them as 'sir' unless told otherwise.

- Maintain eye contact during the interview, but don't stare them out!

- Never slouch in the interview chair. Sit upright at all times and do not fidget.

- When responding to the interview questions avoid any form of waffle or bullsh#t. They will see right through it. Be honest in your responses at all times.

Now let's move on to the next section of the guide where we will look at the selection process for becoming a Para.

CHAPTER 2
THE PARACHUTE REGIMENT SELECTION PROCESS

The selection process for becoming a Para is a long and hard process. The first steps begin with a number of preliminary tests.

PRELIMINARY TESTS

When you first apply to join the Army you will have to undergo a preliminary interview and BARB test, both of which normally take place at the Armed Forces Careers Office. The BARB (British Army Recruit Battery) test is a series of time questions displayed on a computer touch screen. Potential Paras are expected to have higher than average BARB scores. You will notice that I have provided you with an in-depth section within this guide that will go a long way to helping you pass the BARB test.

After you have successfully passed the initial AFCO interview and BARB test, you will then be required to attend the Army Development Selection Centre.

Army Development Selection Centre (ADSC)

All candidates wishing to join the British Army must pass the ADSC, which comprises:

- Full medical by an Army doctor.

- Basic physical tests and aptitude tests

- Introductory 5 minute talk

- Interviews with Army officers

- Other assessable areas

On successfully completion of the initial preliminary tests you will be required to attend the Parachute Regiment Aptitude Course.

Parachute Regiment Assessment Course (PRAC)

The programme below shows the training activities you will undertake whilst attending the Parachute Regiment Assessment Course.

SERIAL	TIMINGS USING 24 HR CLOCK	ACTIVITY	PLACE
01	1230 – 1400	Arrive Helles Barracks, move into accommodation, have lunch, receive initial kit issue.	Helles Barracks, Accommodation
02	1445 – 1715	Medicals, Boot issue and Students Ice Breaker presentations	Vimy Barracks
03	1715 – 1745	Students Ice Breaker presentations	Helles Barracks Soldiers Dining Facility
04	1745 – 1900	Evening meal	Accommodation

SERIAL	TIMINGS USING 24 HR CLOCK	ACTIVITY	PLACE
05	1900 – 2030	Introduction to Barrack routine and demonstration of locker & bed layout and accommodation cleaning tasks	Helles Barracks
06	2030 – 2130	Visit to Helles Barracks HUB/NAAFI facilities	Accommodation
07	0600	Preparation for next day, iron coveralls, polish boots, clean accommodation, arrange locker & bed layout	
08	0600 – 0700	Reveille	Accommodation
09	0700 – 0730	Breakfast	Helles Barracks
10	0730 – 0800	Accommodation inspection. Display locker & bed layout	Accommodation
11	0800 – 0920	Introduction to basic weapon handling - Rifle SA80	Skill at Arms Classroom
12	0920 – 1120	Physical Fitness Assessment. Sit ups (max in 2 mins), Press ups (max in 2 mins), 3.5 mile squadded run at 9min per mile followed by 1.5 mile individual best effort run in 9min 18 to 9min 40 seconds	Gym & Outside area
13	1130 – 1230	Course administration	Accommodation
14	1230 – 1300	Lunch	Helles Barracks
15	1300 – 1400	Lecture - Introduction to the Infantry	Accommodation
16	1400 – 1500	Introduction to Trainasium - aerial obstacle course	Trainasium
17	1500 – 1600	Assessment of morning lesson on basic weapon handling - Rifle SA80	Skill at Arms Classroom

SERIAL	TIMINGS USING 24 HR CLOCK	ACTIVITY	PLACE
18	1600 – 1700	Basic skills test. Write essay. Subject:- on your life as a civilian	Classroom
19	1700 – 1730	Evening Meal	Soldiers Dining Facility
20	1730 – 1830	Basic First Aid Lesson	Accommodation
21	1830 – 1930	Personal administration & preparation for next day	Accommodation
22	1930 – 2030	Visit to Helles Barracks HUB/ NAAFI facilities	Helles Barracks
23	2030 – 2130	Barrack routine & preparation for next day	Accommodation
24	0600– 0700	Reveille - Personal ablutions & Preparation for accommodation inspection	Accommodation
25	0700 – 0730	Breakfast	Helles Barracks
26	0730 – 0800	Accommodation inspection	Accommodation
27	0800 – 0900	Assault Course	Helles Barracks
28	0900 – 1000	Assessment on Basic First Aid Lesson	Accommodation
29	1000 – 1130	Pack Bags/Clean accommo-dation	Accommodation
30	1130 – 1230	Final Interviews	2IC Office
31	1230 – 1300	Lunch	Helles Barracks
32	1300	Dispersal	Minibuses to Darlington Station

You will notice that the above timetable is packed full of assessments. It is imperative that you prepare fully for the PRAC.

Once you have successfully passed the PRAC you will then move onto to Parachute Regiment training.

CHAPTER 3
PREPARING FOR ARMY SELECTION

LEARNING THE VALUES OF THE ARMY

This first step when preparing for any job of any nature is to learn and understand what the organisation you applying to join expect of its employees. The same rule applies to the British Army and when applying to join the Parachute Regiment.

As you can imagine the Army has a set of 'values' in which it every person who works for them must follow and abide by. During the selection process, and in particular the interview, there is a strong chance that you will be asked to explain what the values are and what you understand about them. If I was to ask you the question now "Tell me what the British Army values are?" would you be able to answer it? If not then it is important that you learn them, but more importantly

understand them. As a soldier you will be often required to do things that are other people wouldn't want to do, or would be incapable of doing. As a soldier you will be highly trained and you will be able to carry out your tasks both professionally and competently. However, if the Army did not have these values and it did not have control of its people then things could soon go wrong. As a soldier it can be a difficult task balancing the aggression of combat with the self discipline that is required to perform under immense pressure.

Let's now take a look at the values and what they mean.

The values of the British Army are as follows:

Selfless Commitment – putting other people before you.

Courage – facing up to danger and doing what is right at all times.

Discipline – being able to maintain constant high standards, so that others can rely on you.

Integrity – earning the respect and trust of your work colleagues.

Loyalty – being faithful to your work colleagues and to your duty.

Respect for others – treating others with decency and respect at all times.

Before I go into more detail about each individual value I would recommend that you write each one of them down on a small piece of card or paper and carry it around with you in your wallet or purse. When you get a few spare minutes each day get the card out and read the values. They will soon become second nature to you and you will be able to reel them off quickly.

Selfless Commitment

Every member of the Armed Forces must be totally committed. After all, it is the soldiers and officers who are the foundation of the British Army. You will need to perform to the best of your abilities at all times and you will be required to serve whenever and wherever the Army dictates. Putting the needs of the mission and your team ahead of your own needs is crucial at all times.

Courage

Soldiers are required to go into combat, and that takes unbelievable courage and commitment. Courage creates the strength on which fighting spirit depends. Not only will you need the physical courage that is required but the mental courage also. Even if the task or mission is highly dangerous you will need the strength of character and courage to always do what is right.

Discipline

In order for the Army to perform to the highest of standards then it needs its soldiers and officers to be disciplined. If they are not, then inevitably things will go wrong. Therefore you must obey all lawful orders that are given to you. Probably the most effective form of discipline is that of self discipline. If you are self disciplined then your life in the Army will be far easier. Self discipline brings results and it also brings respect from colleagues and comrades. Without self discipline you will soon land yourself in trouble and you will become more of a hindrance to your Regiment than an asset. Self discipline applies at all times whether you are on operations or not. You will also need self discipline when you are off duty or on leave. When you join the Army you

will become a respected member of society and people will look up to you. In essence you will become a role model for others, and that carries a lot of responsibility. You can't go brawling in the pub or getting yourself on the wrong side of the law. Throughout your Army career you should always look to set a good example.

Integrity

In order to reach the required level of integrity you will need to be trustworthy, honest, reliable, self disciplined and sincere. Integrity is an essential part of Army life and unless you develop and maintain it then people will not trust you. If people do not trust you then the team fails – it's as simple as that.

Loyalty

When I left the Fire Service after 16 years service I received a certificate from the Chief Fire Officer who congratulated me on my 'loyal and devoted service'. Those few words meant a tremendous amount to me as I know that I was totally loyal and devoted to the service throughout my time served. The Army is very similar to the Fire Service in the fact that it requires its men and women to be loyal if it is to achieve its aim of working to the highest standards possible. As you can imagine, the nation and the Army rely on your commitment and support. You must be loyal to your commanders and to your work colleagues and also to your duty. Naturally you will not want to let your team down.

Respect for Others

Having respect for others doesn't just form part of Army life – it also forms part of life in general. During the Army interviews

that you will undergo during selection you will be asked questions that relate to your 'respect for people in positions of authority'. This could be your teachers at school or college or even local Police Officer's. Let me ask you the question now – "what do you think about your teachers at school?" Hopefully your answer will be that you have the highest level of respect for them. Unfortunately many young people do not have the maturity to respect people in positions of authority and this can lead to a failure in discipline. Before you apply to join the Army you must develop a respect for people in positions of authority, and to people in general. No form of bullying, harassment or discrimination will ever be tolerated in the Army and you must be able to treat people with dignity and with respect. If only everybody in society treated everyone with respect then the world would be a much nicer place.

As a soldier you have the exceptional responsibility of using weapons and operating expensive equipment and machinery. In addition to this, you will sometimes have to live and work under extremely difficult conditions. In such circumstances, it is very important that you show the greatest respect for others. Effective teamwork, comradeship and leadership depend on respect and mutual trust.

UNDERSTANDING THE STANDARDS OF CONDUCT

In addition to the values of the British Army it is also important to be aware of the standards of conduct that you will be expected to abide by. Whilst it is not essential to learn these verbatim, it is a good idea to read them and be aware that they do exist. Throughout your career in the Army you will be required to follow strict discipline regulations. Anyone who breaks the rules or who acts in a manner which is damaging

to the reputation of the Army may be subject to an investigation and potentially discipline procedures.

As a soldier serving in the British Army you must:

- Abide by the civil law, wherever you are serving.

- Abide by military law, which includes some additional offences such as insubordination and absence without leave, which are needed to maintain discipline.

- Abide by the laws of armed conflict whenever you are on operations.

- Avoid any activity that undermines your professional ability or puts others at risk, in particular, the misuse of drugs and abuse of alcohol.

- Avoid any behaviour that damages trust and respect between you and others in your team and unit, such as deceit or social misconduct. In particular, you must not commit any form of harassment, bullying or discrimination, whether on grounds of race, gender, religion, sexual orientation, or any other behaviour that could undermine good order and military discipline.

Now that we have taken a brief look into the values and the code of conduct that you will be expected to operate within it is time to explore the selection process.

CHAPTER 4
THE ARMY SCORING CRITERIA

Within this I section of the guide I will provide you with information that relates to how the Army will assess you during the selection process for becoming a Paratrooper. Please note that the assessable criteria for the BARB test and some elements of the ADSC and PRAC are different. The criteria that I am going to provide you with during this section of the guide relates to your own personal attributes, qualities and also your knowledge of the Army and your chosen career in the Parachute Regiment. This information will act as a very good foundation for your preparation. If you are capable of providing the Army selecting officers with what they are looking for then your chances of success will greatly increase.

The marking sheet used to assess your abilities covers a number of different assessable areas. The following list is a selection of some of the criteria used:

• Personal turnout;

- Sociability;
- Emotional maturity and stability;
- Drive and determination to succeed;
- Physically robust;
- Experience of being self-reliant;
- Reactions to social discipline;
- Experience of and reaction to regimentation and routine;
- Knowledge and experience of Army life;
- Motivation to join the Army;
- Personal circumstances.

This list is not exhaustive and there will be other areas that the Army will be assessing you on during the interviews and written tests. However, having an understanding of the qualities you need to demonstrate throughout selection will improve your chances of success dramatically.

In order to provide you with a greater understanding of what is required I will now go into more detail about each specific area.

PERSONAL TURNOUT

The Army are looking for you to be smartly dressed when you attend the AFCO, the ADSC, PRAC and also during your interview. They also want to see that you have made an effort to present yourself positively. When you attend the careers office, whether it is for an interview or a careers presentation, always make sure you wear a formal outfit such as a suit or shirt and tie. Whilst this is not essential it will allow you to score higher in the area of 'personal turnout'.

Many people will stroll into the careers office wearing jeans and trainers. Make an effort to stand out for the right reasons and this certainly will work in your favour. Those people who turn up to the Armed Forces Careers Office dressed untidy and unwashed will score poorly. Throughout the duration of the guide I will make reference to the importance of dressing smart and making the effort to present yourself in a positive, motivated and professional manner.

Tips for scoring high in personal turnout

- Make sure your shoes are clean and polished;

- Shirt, trousers and tie for males and a smart formal outfit for females;

- Ensure your clothes are ironed and not creased;

- Work on your personal hygiene and overall appearance. Make sure your nails are clean!

- Stand tall and be confident;

- Don't slouch in the interview chair.

SOCIABILITY

This section assesses your ability to mix well with people. The Army want to know that you are socially confident and outgoing. It is also important that you have a good sense of humour. They want to know that you can fit in well with the Army way of life and that you have no problems with communal living.

When you join the Army you will be required to live in accommodation that comprises of many people. As you progress up through the ranks the amount of people that you'll be

required to live with will decrease, until you eventually get a room on your own! Some people find it very difficult to socialise with others and these are not the type of people the Army want to recruit. They need people who will fit into the team spirit and whom have no problem with communicating with others. Those applicants who come across as quiet or shy will not score well in the area of sociability. At no point during selection should you be brash, abrasive or not a team player.

Tips for scoring high in sociability

- During the interviews provide examples of where you have mixed well with others. This may be through youth organisations such as the Scouts etc;

- If you have played team sports then this will be an advantage;

- Tell the interviewer that you will have no problem with communal living. Communal living is living with other people. You may be in a room of up to thirty other people whilst in your training, so they want to know that you are comfortable with this;

- Smile and laugh where appropriate – a sense of humour is a must but never be over bearing or over confident. Never 'back chat' or be disrespectful to the recruiting officers and staff.

EMOTIONAL MATURITY AND STABILITY

The Army want to see that you are mature for your age and that you are even tempered and well balanced. They don't want people who are aggressive or who come across with a bad attitude. They want to see that you have coped well with

the ups and downs of life so far and you may find that they ask you questions on any difficult areas of life that you have had to deal with. They want to know that you will adapt well to the change in lifestyle when you join the Army and that you can cope in highly stressful situations. The Army will also be looking for you to be mature for your age and that there are no signs of depression or anxiety. They will also be assessing your ability to cope well with unfamiliar surroundings and that you will not become homesick during training.

Tips for scoring high in emotional maturity and stability

- During the interviews and during discussions with the Armed Forces Careers Officer advisor try to provide examples of where you have dealt well with difficult situations in your life in a positive and mature manner;

- Try to be upbeat and positive about the future;

- Don't be overconfident or macho.

DRIVE AND DETERMINATION TO SUCCEED

The Army want to know that you have a sense of purpose in your life. They will be looking for a pattern of achievement, either through school or at work, and for evidence that you are not easily deflected from your goals and aspirations. They want to see that you are a competitive person who is highly motivated to succeed. You will recall at the beginning of this guide how much emphasis I put on perseverance. Drive and determination are very similar to perseverance in that you have the ability to keep working hard and improving yourself until you achieve success.

Those applicants who show signs that they give up easily or have no goals aspirations will score poorly in the area of drive and determination to succeed.

Tips for scoring high in drive and determination to succeed

- Provide examples of where you have achieved. This might be educational qualifications, courses that you have attended or even sporting achievements;

- Be positive about joining the Army and tell them that nothing is going to stop you from succeeding. If you don't pass this time then you will look for ways to improve for the next time you apply;

- Demonstrate that your ambition and sense of purpose is to join the Army and become a professional and competent soldier.

PHYSICALLY ROBUST

The Army want to see that you engage in outdoor activities and that you have some experience in playing team sports. Being physically active is important and if you are strong and free from injuries and weakness then this will be an advantage during selection. If you are not involved in any form of team sports then I advise that you start straight away. It is very easy to become involved in team sports as there are so many to choose from. Examples of team sports include football, hockey, rugby and basketball.

Those applicants who provide evidence that they are generally isolated individuals who spend too much time at home on the computer or watching TV will score lower than those who are physically active.

Tips for scoring high in physical robustness

- Be involved in competitive team sports;

- Be an active outdoor type person;

- Attend the gym and carry out light weight exercises and workouts.

EXPERIENCE OF BEING SELF RELIANT

The Army want to know that you can handle the pressure of living away from home. If you have travelled or have been on camps where you have had to 'rough it' then this would be an advantage. Basically they want to know that you can look after yourself without the help of your parents or home comforts.

If you have no experience whatsoever of being self reliant then I advise that you take steps to improve your experience of this area. For example, there is nothing to stop you from going camping for the weekend or joining the Army Cadets where you will be able to gain experience of this important attribute.

Tips for scoring high in being self reliant

- Provide examples of where you have been away from home for short or long periods of time;

- Tell the interviewer that you enjoy travelling and being away from home. Remember that it is important to provide examples of where you have already done this.

- Tell the interviewer that you are looking forward to leaving home to join the Army and face the challenges that it presents;

- Provide examples of where you have had to fend for yourself or where you have been away camping.

REACTIONS TO SOCIAL DISCIPLINE

The Army want to see that you have a positive attitude towards authority. People in authority include the police, your parents, teachers and even your boss at work. When you join the Army you will be taking orders from senior officers and they want to know that you have no problem with authority.

There is a strong possibility that the interviewer will ask you questions that relate to your attitude to education and your teachers. At no point should you be negative about your teachers or about people whom are in positions of authority. If you are disrespectful or negative about these people then there is a strong possibility that the Army selection officers will take a dim view on your attitude. For example, I have been aware of applicants who complain during the Army Interview that their teachers were rubbish at their job and that everyone in the class would always laugh at them. As you can imagine, those applicants do not progress any further during the selection process.

Tips for scoring high in social discipline

- Try to provide examples of where you have carried out orders, either at work or at school;

- Tell the interviewer that you respect authority, providing you do of course, and that you see it as an important aspect of life. You do not have a problem with taking orders from anyone, even if they are the opposite sex to you.

EXPERIENCE AND REACTION TO REGIMENT AND ROUTINE

When you join the Army you will lose much of your personal freedom. During your initial training there will be many

restrictions placed upon you in terms of leave and your general freedom. You won't be given the time to do all of the things that you usually do whilst at home. Therefore, the Army want to see that you have the ability to cope with this added pressure and disciplined routine.

You must try to demonstrate during the selection process that you have already experienced some form of routine and that you are capable of following rules and regulations. This could simply be by having some form of disciplined routine at home, whereby you are required to clean the house and carry out the ironing for a few hours every week.

Tips for scoring high in experience of and reaction to regimentation and routine

- Provide examples of where you have lost your personal freedom, either during your upbringing, at school or during work. Maybe you have had to work unsociable hours or had to dedicate time and effort into your educational studies?

- Tell the interviewer that you fully understand that you will lose your personal freedom when you join the Army and that it won't be a problem for you.

- Implement some form of routine into your preparation strategy for joining the Army. Set out your action plan early on and follow it rigidly.

KNOWLEDGE AND EXPERIENCE OF ARMY LIFE

Having knowledge of Army life can be achieved in a number of ways. If you have been a member of any youth organisations then this will be an obvious advantage. Youth organisations include the Scouts, Army Cadets, Air Training

Corps or Sea Cadets etc. If a member of your family or a friend is a member of the Armed Forces then you can also gain knowledge through them simply by asking them questions about their job and life within the Armed Forces. It is also important to gain knowledge of Army life by reading your recruitment literature and visiting the Army website if you have access to the Internet.

Another fantastic way to gain invaluable knowledge of how the Army operates and its equipment is to grab yourself a copy of the book entitled 'The British Army: A Pocket Guide'. This book usually sells for approximately £5.99 and it fits easily into your pocket. Any spare moments you have during the day you can get the book out and start reading about vital facts that relate to the British Army.

Tips for scoring high in knowledge and experience of Army life

- Speak to any friends or relatives who are members of the Armed Forces and ask them what it is like. Gain as much information as possible from the Armed Forces Careers Office staff and also through your recruitment literature;

- Find out as much as possible about the training you will undertake when you join the Army for your chosen career and also your initial recruit training;

- Consider visiting an Army establishment or museum. These are great places to learn about Army life.

- Consider joining a youth organisation such as the Scouts or cadets to gain some experience of a disciplined service.

MOTIVATION TO JOIN THE ARMY

The Army want to see that it is your own decision to join and that you haven't been pushed into it by friends or your family. Joining the Army to become a soldier first and a tradesman second is also important. They want to see that you have been pulled by the attractions of the Army as opposed to being pushed into them. If you are successful in your application the Army will be investing a tremendous amount of time, energy and finances into your training and development. The last thing they want is that you decide it's not for you. Once you join the Army you will have to serve 28 days in training. After the 28th day you can apply in writing to leave. If you're under 18 when you join, you have six months to let the Army know your decision and three months if over 18. Once this time has passed you are committed to serving your contract so you must be 100% certain that it's for you.

Tips for scoring high in motivation to join the Army

- Always present a positive attitude towards joining when you visit the Armed Forces Careers Office and also whilst attending the ADSC. This choice of career should be something that you considered very carefully about and you have been working very hard to make sure that you pass;

- Try to think about what attracts you to the Army and tell the interviewer during selection.

PERSONAL CIRCUMSTANCES

The Army will want to know that you have the support of your family and/or your partner. They also want to see that you are free from any detracting circumstances such as

financial difficulties. If you are in financial difficulty then this could have a negative effect on your mental health during training. They will assess your personal circumstances during selection and also at the ADSC interview.

Tips for scoring high in personal circumstances

- Speak to your parents and your partner (if applicable) about your choice of career. Ask them for their support;

- If they do not support you or they are concerned about you joining then I would recommend that you take them along to the careers office so that the Army Forces Careers Officer can talk to them about Army life and answer any questions that they may have. It is imperative that you have their full support.

CHAPTER 5
HOW TO PASS THE INTERVIEWS FOR JOINING THE PARACHUTE REGIMENT

During the Army selection process you will be required to sit a number of interviews both at the AFCO, the ADSC and the PRAC. The information that I have provided within this section of the guide will assist you during your preparation for all of these interviews.

The Army will use a set marking sheet for your interviews and the questions will be based around a number of specific criteria. The questions will vary from interview to interview but the core elements are designed to assess whether you are suitable to join the service. The following is a list of areas you may be asked questions on during your Army interview and I would recommend that you use these as a basis for your preparation:

- The reasons why you want to join the Army.

- The reasons why you have chosen the Parachute Regiment.

- What information you already know about the Army, the Regiment and the lifestyle and training.

- Information bout your hobbies and interests including sporting activities.

- Any personal responsibilities that you currently have at home, at school or at work.

- Information about your family and what they think about you joining the Army. Do they support you?

- Information based around your initial application form.

- Your experience of work and education and whether or not you have had any responsibility at home or work.

- Your emotional stability and your maturity.

- Your drive and determination to succeed.

- Any experience you have of working as part of a team.

- Your attitude towards physical exercise and team sports.

- Having a positive reaction to the disciplined environment.

- Your knowledge of life within the Army and in particular the Parachute Regiment.

Over the next few pages I have provided you with a number of sample interview questions and responses. These will act as a good basis for your preparation. However, it is important to point out at this stage the responses you provide during the interview should be based solely on your own experiences and opinions.

SAMPLE INTERVIEW QUESTION NUMBER 1

Why do you want to join the Army?

This is an almost guaranteed question during your Army interview so there should be no reason why you can't answer it in a positive manner. Try to display motivation when answering questions of this nature. The Army are looking for people who want to become a professional member of their team and who understand the Army way of life. By studying your Army recruitment literature and the Army website you will understand what service life is all about. You want to be a member of the British Army and you are attracted to what it has to offer. If you have been pushed into joining by your family then you shouldn't be applying.

Sample response to question number 1

Why do you want to join the Army?

"I have wanted to join the Army for a number of years now and feel that I have now reached a part of my life where I am ready to commit to the service. Having studied the Army recruitment literature and visited the Army website, I am impressed by the professionalism and standards the service sets itself.

I would like a career that is fulfilling, challenging and rewarding and I believe that the Army would provide all of these. I enjoy keeping physically fit and active and believe that given the right training I would make a great team member. I am also very much attracted to the fact that the Army offers a wide choice of careers. I have a massive desire to join the elite Parachute Regiment. The reason why I want to join the Regiment is because I believe I have exceptional qualities that would be suited to this career. I am extremely physically fit and enjoy very tough challenges. I have held a keen

interest in the Regiment from a young age and have taken the decision to apply very seriously.

The fact that I would be improving my education and ending up with a trade is just another example of why I want to join the service. I have seriously considered the implications that joining a service such as the Army would have on both my personal life and social life and discussed these with my family. They have given me their full support and commitment in helping me to achieve my goal of joining the Army.'

SAMPLE INTERVIEW QUESTION NUMBER 2

What does your family think of you wanting to join the Army?
Again, you are likely to be asked a question surrounding your family background and what they think about you wanting to join the Army. It is important that your family support you in your decision.

If they have any doubts about you joining the service then you may wish to consider taking them along to the AFCO so they can ask any questions or raise any concerns that they may have. When answering questions such as this it is important that you are honest and tell the truth. If your family have any concerns then share them with the careers officer, who will then be able to advise you on the best way for your family/partner to overcome any fears they may have.

Sample response to question number 2

What does your family think of you wanting to join the Army?
'I have discussed the issue with them in depth and also shown them all of the Army recruitment literature to try to dampen any fears that they may have.

They were initially concerned about me joining but they gave me their full support after I told them everything I know about the training I will go through and the conditions I will serve under. They are aware that the Army has a good reputation and this has helped them to further understand why I want to join. They have seen how enthusiastic I am about wanting to join the Army and know that it will be great for me. I have also discussed the issue with my partner and he/she is extremely supportive. They are all looking forward to hopefully seeing me at my passing out parade if I am successful and therefore I have their full backing.'

SAMPLE INTERVIEW QUESTION NUMBER 3

How do you think you will cope with Army life in relation to the discipline and being part of a military organisation?

When you join the Army you will be joining a military organisation that has set procedures, standards and discipline codes. To some people this will come as a shock and the Army want to know that you are prepared for this change in lifestyle. They are investing time, effort and resources into your training so they want to know that you can cope with their way of life.

When answering this type of question you need to demonstrate both your awareness of what Army life involves and also your positive attitude towards the disciplined environment. Study the recruitment literature and visit the Army website to get a feel for the type of training you will be going through.

Sample response to question number 3

How do you think you will cope with Army life in relation to the discipline and being part of a military organisation?

'Having read the information available to me about the Army way of life I think I would cope very well. I know that I will find it difficult at times but believe I have both the maturity and stability to succeed and become a competent member of the team. The very nature of the Army means that it requires a disciplined workforce. Without that discipline things can go wrong. If I am successful and do not carry out my duties professionally then I could endanger somebody's life. I understand why discipline is required and believe I would cope with it well. I understand that being in the Army isn't a 9-5 job, but instead you must take on tasks whenever required.

In order to prepare for the training I have already integrated routine and self discipline into my life. For example, I have been getting up at 6am every weekday morning to go running and I have started carrying out daily household tasks such as hovering, cleaning and ironing. At the start of my preparation for joining the Army I made myself an action plan that would focus my mind on what I needed to do in order to improve.'

SAMPLE INTERVIEW QUESTION NUMBER 4

How do you think you will cope with being away from home and losing your personal freedom?

This type of question is one that needs to be answered positively. There is only one correct answer to this question and you need to demonstrate that you have considered the consequences of leaving home and are fully aware of what is involved. If you have any experience of being away from home then you should state this in your response. Try to think of occasions when you have been away for periods of time and tell them that it wasn't an issue.

Have you ever been a part of any youth organisations? If you have then this will undoubtedly go in your favour. Giving an example is far better than just saying you will be able to cope.

Sample response to question number 4

How do you think you will cope with being away from home and losing your personal freedom?

'Having already had experience of being away from home, I believe I would cope extremely well. Whilst serving with the Scouts a few years ago I was introduced to the Army way of life and fully understand what it is like to be away from home. I actually enjoy being away from home and I can't wait to get started if I am successful during selection. I understand however that the training is difficult and intense and I am fully prepared for this. I am confident that I will cope with the change in lifestyle very well and I am looking forward to the challenge if I am accepted.'

SAMPLE INTERVIEW QUESTION NUMBER 5

Are you involved in any sporting activities and how do you keep yourself fit?

When answering questions based around your own physical fitness you need to be honest but bear in mind the following points:

Although you don't have to be super fit to join the Army, you do need to have a very good level of physical fitness in order to join the Parachute Regiment. The Army, just like the other Armed Forces, pride themselves on their ability to work as an effective team unit. Those people who engage in active team sports are more likely to be competent team members. If you play a team sport then this will be a good thing to

tell them. If you don't then it may be a good idea to go and join one! Regardless of the above points, remember that if you don't do any physical activity whatsoever then you will score low in this area. Make sure you partake in some form of physical activity. During the ADSC and the PRAC you will be required to carry out a 1.5 mile run which should be your 'best effort'. The Army has realised that those people who cannot complete the run in a set time are far more likely to suffer from injury during the initial training course. Start running now so that you can easily pass the forthcoming physical tests.

Sample response to question number 5

Are you involved in any sporting activities and how do you keep yourself fit?

'Yes I am. I currently play in the local Rugby team and have been doing that for a number of years now. Maintaining a good level of fitness is something I enjoy. In fact, recently I have increased my fitness levels by going swimming three times a week. I'm aware that during the recruit training course I will be pushed to my limits so I need to be prepared for that. I believe the fact that I play team sports will help me get through my training.

I enjoy playing in a Rugby team because when we are being beaten by another team everyone always pulls together and we work hard to try to win the game back. After the game we all meet in the club bar for a drink and chat about the game. Keeping fit is important to me and something that I want to continue doing throughout my career if I am successful in joining the Army.'

SAMPLE INTERVIEW QUESTION NUMBER 6

How do you think you will fit into a team environment?

Once again, it would be a positive thing if you can demonstrate you have experience of working in a team. Maybe you have experience of working in a sporting team or need to work as a team in your current job? Try to think of examples where you have already been working in a team environment and if you can provide an example where the team achieved something then even better. Structure your answer around your own experiences and also around your knowledge of the fact that the Army needs to work as an effective team unit in order for it to complete its tasks both safely and on time.

Sample response to question number 6

How do you think you will fit into a team environment?

'I have experience of working in a team and I really enjoyed it, so I know I would fit in well. I play for my local rugby team and it is important that everybody gels together in order to win our games. The real test for the team is when we are being beaten and I always try to rally the team together and get us motivated to win back the points we have lost. I understand that the Army needs to work together effectively as a team to get the right result. If the team doesn't perform then people's lives can be put at risk. Being an effective part of the team also means that I would have to train hard and keep up my competency levels, which I believe I would do well.

With my experience of team sports and having the ability to pull a team together when the chips are down, I think I would be a great asset to the Army team.'

SAMPLE INTERVIEW QUESTION NUMBER 7

What do you do in your spare time?
With questions of this nature the Army recruitment staff are looking to see if you use your leisure time wisely. Your response will tell them a lot about your attitude and motivation. We all know that some people spend their spare time doing nothing or watching TV and playing computer games. When you join the Army you won't have much time to sit around and do nothing. The Army will want to hear that you are active and doing worthwhile things during your spare time. For example, if you are involved in any sports, outdoor activities or are part of any youth organisation such as the Army Cadets then these are good things to tell them. You may also be involved in voluntary work or charity work and once again these will work in your favour if mentioned at interview.

If you currently do very little with your spare time then now is a good time to make a lifestyle change. Embark on a fitness routine or join an activity club or organisation.

Sample response to question number 7

What do you do in your spare time?
'During my spare time I like to keep active, both physically and mentally. I enjoy visiting the gym three times a week and I have a structured workout that I try to vary every three months to keep my interest levels up. I'm also currently doing a part-time study course in Art, which is one of my hobbies. I'm also a member of the local Army Cadets, which is an evening's commitment every week and the occasional weekend.

Of course, I know when it is time to relax and usually do this by either listening to music or playing snooker with my

friends, but overall I'm quite an active person. I certainly don't like sitting around doing nothing. I understand that if I'm successful at joining the Army there will be plenty of things to do in the evenings to keep me occupied such as the gym and other various social events.'

SAMPLE INTERVIEW QUESTION NUMBER 8

Can you tell us about any personal achievements you have experienced during your life so far?

Having achieved something in your life demonstrates that you have the ability to see things through to the end. It also shows that you are motivated and determined to succeed. The Army want to see evidence that you can achieve, as there is a greater chance of you completing the initial recruit course if you have a history of this. Try to think of examples where you have succeeded or achieved something relevant in your life. Some good examples of achievements are as follows:

- Duke of Edinburgh's Award;

- A-levels or educational qualifications;

- Team or individual sports awards/trophies/medals;

- Raising money for charity.

Obviously you will have your own achievements that you will want to add in your response.

Sample response to question number 8

Can you tell us about any personal achievements you have experienced during your life so far?

'So far in my life I have managed to achieve a number of things that I am proud of. To begin with, I recently worked

hard to achieve my 'GCSE' results, which enabled me to go on to further education and study my choice of subject. Without these grades I would not have been able to do that.

About a year ago the football team that I play in won the league trophy for the second year running, which is another one of my more recent achievements.

However, my most memorable achievement to date is managing to raise £1,000 for a local charity. I worked hard and ran a marathon in order to raise the money. I was particularly proud of this achievement because It meant the charity I ran for were able to purchase some important items of equipment that could be used to treat some of their patients.'

SAMPLE INTERVIEW QUESTION NUMBER 9

What are your strengths?

This is a common interview question, which is relatively easy to answer. The problem with it is that many people use the same response. It is quite an easy thing to tell the interviewer that you are dedicated and the right person for the job. However, it is a different thing backing it up with evidence!

If you are asked this type of question make sure you are positive during your response and show that you actually mean what you are saying. Then, back your answer up with examples of when you have demonstrated a strength that you say you have. For example, if you tell the panel that you are a motivated person, then back it up with an event in your life where you achieved something through sheer motivation and determination.

Sample response to question number 9

What are your strengths?

'To begin with I am a determined *person* who likes to see *things through to the end. For example, I recently ran a marathon for charity. I'd never done this kind of thing before and found it very hard work, but I made sure I completed the task. Another strength of mine is that I'm always looking for ways to improve myself. As an example, I was preparing for the Army selection process by performing lots of mock mathematical tests.*

I noticed that I was getting a number of questions wrong. In order to improve I decided to get some personal tuition at my college to ensure that I could pass this part of the selection process. Finally, I would say that one of my biggest strengths is that I'm a great team player. I really enjoy working in a team environment and achieving things through a collaborative approach. For example, I play in a local rugby team and we recently won the league trophy for the first time since the club was established some 50 years ago.'

SAMPLE INTERVIEW QUESTION NUMBER 10

What is your biggest weakness?

Now there's a question! If we were all totally honest with ourselves we could probably write a whole list of weaknesses. Now I wouldn't advise that you reel off a whole list of weaknesses in your interview as you could do yourself a lot of harm. Conversely, those people who say that they don't have any weaknesses are probably not telling the truth.

If you are asked a question of this nature then it is important that you give at least one weakness. The trick here is to make the weakness sound like a strength. For example, a

person may say that one of their weaknesses is that their own personal standards are too high sometimes and they expect this of others. Or another one is that a person doesn't know when to relax. They are always on the go achieving and making things happen when they should take more time out to relax and recuperate.

Sample response to question number 10

What is your biggest weakness?

'That's a difficult question but I know that I do have a particular weakness. The standards that I always set myself are quite high and unfortunately I get frustrated when other peoples aren't. For example, I am hardly ever late for anything and believe that punctuality is important. However, if I'm left waiting for other people who are late I usually have to say something to them when they finally arrive, which isn't always a good thing. I need to understand that not everyone is the same and let some things go over my head.'

SAMPLE INTERVIEW QUESTION NUMBER 11

Can you tell me what you have learnt about the Parachute Regiment?

Once again, an almost guaranteed question so make sure you have prepared for it fully. When preparing for this type of question I would recommend that you visit the Army website and also study carefully your recruitment literature.

I would also recommend that you find out the type and length of training you would be expected to undertake as a Paratrooper. This information will be available through your Armed Forces Careers advisor. Use the example that follows to create your own response relevant to your own chosen

career. You may even wish to look at other avenues or research to improve your knowledge and further demonstrate your determination to succeed.

Sample response to question number 11

Can you tell me what you have learnt about the Parachute Regiment?

"The Parachute Regiment forms the Airborne Infantry element of 16 Air Assault Brigade. The role of the Regiment is to operate with minimal or no support behind enemy lines and against other superior forces.

On the 22nd June 1940, Winston Churchill called for the formation of an elite Corps of troops.... the PARAS. Following Churchill's wishes for "a corps of at least 5,000 parachute troops, suitably organised and equipped" a Parachute Training School was established at Ringway Airport near Manchester and No 2 Commando was chosen for the first training in parachute duties; the regiment quickly growing into the 11th Special Air Service Battalion and ultimately, on the 1st August 1942, the Parachute Regiment. By the end of WW2, the Regiment comprised of 17 battalions.

1 Para form part of the Special Forces Support group who provides specialist infantry support to Special Forces, such as the SAS, anywhere in the world. 2 Para are the Second Battalion and form part of 16 Air Assault Brigade. They are based in Colchester, Essex. 3 Para are the 3rd Battalion The Parachute Regiment and form part of 16 Air assault Brigade. Once again they based in Colchester, Essex. The 4th Battalion, The Parachute Regiment (4 PARA) is the reserve parachute battalion which has its headquarters in Pudsey, West Yorkshire.

If I am successful in passing selection, I must go through

Pre-Parachute Selection which is run by Pegasus Company (P Coy) at the Infantry Training Centre in Catterick, North Yorkshire.

During Test Week I would be required to pass 8 tests, held over 7 days which include:

10 miler - carrying 35lb bergen and a rifle, to be completed in1 hour 50 minutes or under.

Trainasium - An assault course designed to test a candidate's head for heights.

Log Race - 8-man team carrying a 60kg log over 1.9km.

2 Mile March - carrying 35lb bergen, food, water and a rifle, to be completed in 18 minutes or under.

Steeplechase - 1.8 mile cross-country course featuring water obstacles and an assault course.

Milling - Milling tests if the recruit as the aggression and determination required of a Paratrooper. Recruits must aggressively pummel their opponent whilst wearing boxing gloves and head guard.

Endurance March - 20 miles carrying 35lb bergen, water, food and a rifle, to be completed in 4 hours or under (TA recruits do not do the endurance march).

Stretcher Race - 16-man teams carry a 175 lb stretcher over 5 miles."

SAMPLE INTERVIEW QUESTION NUMBER 12

What qualities do you think you need to be a good team player?
The Army needs effective and competent team players. If you already have some experience of working in a team

environment then this will work in your favour. Try to think of examples where you have already successfully contributed to a team task either at work or during your education. There are many different qualities required to work as an effective team player. Here are just a few:

- Enthusiastic;

- A good communicator;

- Motivated;

- Supportive of the other team members;

- Providing other team members with encouragement;

- Determined to complete the task;

- Professional and competent;

- Always focused on the wider team objective.

Now take a look at the following sample response to this question.

Sample response to question number 12

What qualities do you think you need to be a good team player?
'First of all I believe a team player must be focused purely on the task that the team is trying to achieve. You must always be professional and supportive of the other team members. For example, if one of the team members is struggling then you should try to help them and support them with their role within the team. It is important as a team player to listen to the brief or details of the task and to communicate properly with everyone else in the team. You must always put the needs of the team before your own and be totally committed to completing the task in hand.'

SAMPLE INTERVIEW QUESTION NUMBER 13

What contact have you had with the Army during your application and what have you done to find out about Army life?
Those applicants who are serious about a career in the Army will have gone out of their way to find out about the service and what it involves. The Army recruitment staff will want to see evidence that you have taken steps to speak to people who are already serving and that you have researched the organisation effectively. It is important that you are 100% committed to joining and that you are fully aware of the challenge that lies ahead of you.

The following is a sample response to this question.

Sample response to question number 13

What contact have you had with the Army during your application and what have you done to find out about Army life?
'During my preparation I have carried out lots of research into the Army, and in particular the Parachute Regiment, so that I am fully aware of the challenge that lies ahead of me. To begin with I have studied my recruitment literature in depth and I have also spent plenty of time browsing the Army recruitment website. I have also obtained a copy of the British Army Pocket Guide which has taught me lots about the service, the regiments and the equipment. More recently I spent a couple of hours at my local Army establishment where I managed to speak to serving soldiers and officers about their role and the job. I found this an invaluable insight. All of this research and reading has made me more excited about joining. I cannot wait to get started if I am successful.'

SAMPLE INTERVIEW QUESTION NUMBER 14

What are the values of the British Army?

During one of the very first stages of this guide I made reference to the Army values. Every soldier and officer is expected to abide by these important values and therefore it is not unreasonable for the Army to expect you to know them when you apply. You are likely to be asked a question that relates to the values during the ADSC so make sure you know them and what each one of them means. Here is a sample response to this question.

Sample response to question number 14

What are the values of the British Army?

'The values of the British Army are a selfless commitment, courage, discipline, integrity, loyalty and respect for others. As a soldier you have to be prepared to carry out tasks that others don't have to. It is important to be strong and aggressive in battle but to also behave properly and demonstrate self control at all times. Army soldiers and officers have to be aggressive and strong in battle, yet behave properly and show self-control all of the time. Being courageous means facing up to danger and doing what is right at all times. Discipline means having the ability to maintain constant high standards, so that others can rely on you. Integrity means earning the respect and trust of your work colleagues. Loyalty is being faithful to your work colleagues and to your duty and having respect for others means treating everybody with respect and dignity at all times.'

SAMPLE INTERVIEW QUESTION NUMBER 15

What are you currently doing in order to prepare for your training?

Whilst this question should be generally easy to answer, it does end up throwing many applicants. Most people who apply to join the Army will do little or no preparation for basic training until they have received confirmation that they have passed the ADSC and PRAC. However, if you can show the Army Development Selection Officer at ADSC and at the PRAC that you are already preparing for basic training then this will impress them. Here is a sample response to assist you.

Sample response to question number 15

What are you currently doing in order to prepare for your training?
'Although I haven't yet passed selection I have been preparing thoroughly for my basic training as I want to ensure I am fully prepared. To begin with I have created a timetable of preparation which makes sure I work on my weak areas and my overall fitness. Every weekday I am up at 6am and I embark on a 4 mile run. This is so that I can get used to the early starts and so that I can improve my fitness levels. Half way round my run I always make sure I stop and carry out 50 press ups and 50 sit ups. When I get home from work I then sit down for an hour and work on my knowledge of the Army and the branch that I am applying for. Every other day I work on my aptitude test ability and I make sure I read a good quality newspaper so that I am up to date with Army operations and the more important current affairs issues. Finally, I have been working on my household skills such as ironing and cleaning.'

SAMPLE INTERVIEW QUESTION NUMBER 16

Tell me about your educational exam results. Were you satis-fied with them and what did you think of your teachers and your school?

Many people leave school without the grades that they want. I was one of them! However, it's my opinion that what you do following your exam results that's the most important thing. Despite only achieving three GCSE's at grade C or above I went on to achieve many qualifications after my initial school education was over. Apart from many Fire Service qualifications I more recently achieve a Diploma in Management and various health and safety qualifications. The point I am trying to make here is that you can still achieve many things in life despite poor educational qualifications.

This question is designed to see what you personally think about your results and also your attitude to your education and people (teachers), who are in positions of authority. If you didn't get the results that you wanted then just say so. However, it is important to tell the interviewer what you plan to do about them and what your plans are for the future. When I passed Armed Forces selection many years ago I had a 6 month wait before I could start my basic training. The Warrant Officer at the AFCO advised that I embarked on an educational foundation course at college for the 6 month period whilst I waited to commence my basic training. I took his advice and I am glad that I did. Whilst responding to this interview question be positive about the future and tell the interviewer what you are currently doing to improve you academic skills. Tell them how hard you have been working for the BARB tests and what steps you have taken to study and prepare for Army selection.

The second part of the question is very important. As I discussed at the beginning of the guide the Army will be

assessing your reaction to discipline and regimentation. Those candidates who are disrespectful to their parents, teachers of people in positions of authority are very unlikely to pass selection. Be careful what you say and always demonstrate a mature and professional image to the interviewer.

Sample response to question number 16

Tell me about your educational exam results. Were you satisfied with them and what did you think of your teachers and your school?

'I did ok on the majority of exams but I wasn't satisfied with my Maths result. I know I could have done better. However, since my results I've working hard to improve my skills in this area and I have embarked on an evening course which will hopefully gain me a better grade. I am a determined person and I'm always looking to improve my skills. One of my strengths is that I can see what I need to work on and I always make sure I work hard to make the necessary improvements.

In relation to my teachers and my school I have a lot of respect for them. The teachers are in positions of authority and it is important to respect that.'

INTERVIEW QUESTION NUMBER 17

What contract will you be under if you are successful and what are your discharge option?

This question is sometimes asked so that the Army can be certain you are fully aware of the commitment you will need to make. If you don't know the minimum contract terms and the discharge options then make sure you find out before you attend your interview. Here is a sample response to this question.

Sample response to question number 17

What contract will you be under if you are successful and what are your discharge option?

'Because I am over 18 years old my contract time is four years and three months. If I want to leave after this point then I will have to give 12 months notice in writing. If I wish to stay on after the initial four years and three months then I can leave at anytime providing that I give the 12 months notice in writing. I am aware that the maximum I can serve is 22 years.

With regards to discharge options I have to serve 28 days initial training. After the 28th day I can write to the Army and request to leave. After this time I am committed to serving my contract.'

TOP INTERVIEW TIPS FOR PASSING THE INTERVIEWS

- When you walk into the interview room stand up straight with your shoulders back. Project an image of confidence;

- Don't sit down in the interview chair until invited to do so;

- Sit with your hands resting on your knees, palms downwards. It is OK to use your hands expressively but don't overdo it;

- Don't slouch in the chair;

- Speak up and be positive;

- Smile, be happy and have a sense of humour;

- Dress as smart as you can and take a pride in your appearance. If you don't have a suit make sure you wear a shirt and tie at the very least.

- Improve your personal administration. By this I mean your personal hygiene and cleanliness. Make sure you have washed and your hands and nails are clean.

- Make sure you have researched both the Army life and your chosen career/careers. This is very important.

- During the interview do not be negative or disrespectful towards your teachers, parents or people in positions of authority. Remember that you are applying to join a disciplined service.

- Go the extra mile and learn a little bit about the Army's history if you get time. When the panel ask you 'What can you tell us about the Army?' you will be able to demonstrate that you have made an effort to look into their history as well as their modern day activities;

- Be respectful and courteous towards the interview panel. At the end of your response to each question finish off with either 'Sir' or 'Ma'am' or as otherwise instructed.

- Ask positive questions at the end of the interview. Try not to ask questions such as "How much leave will I get?" or "How often do I get paid?"

- If you are unsure about a question don't waffle. If you do not know the answer then it is OK to say so. Move on to the next question and put it behind you.

- Finally, believe in yourself and be confident. A positive attitude will bring positive results!

CHAPTER 6
THE BRITISH ARMY
RECRUIT BATTERY TEST

So far within the guide we have covered a large number of topics that relate to your preparation and mental approach towards the selection process. Over the next few sections we will set to work on improving your ability to pass the different stages.

One of the initial stages of the selection process will see a requirement for you to sit the British Army Recruit Battery Test. The test is more commonly known as the 'BARB test' and it has been in use for many years. It is a tried and tested method that the Army will use to determine what career(s) you are most likely to be suited for. It is important that you aim for the highest score possible on the test and this can only be achieved through 'deliberate' and 'repetitive' practice.

The pass mark for the BARB test is currently 26 although you will need to confirm this with your local Armed Forces

Careers Office. This effectively means that you must get 26 questions correct, but as I mentioned earlier don't just settle for a pass. You need to achieve as high a score as possible as this will give you more career options depending on your academic results.

Work hard at practising the tests within this guide and also within the BARB booklet when you receive it from the AFCO. Don't just sit back like so many people do – practise hard and make sure you pass. Your choice of trade will be dependant upon the score you achieve during the BARB test. Basically, the higher your score, the more career options you will have. This is a good incentive therefore for you to work hard and prepare fully.

It is also important that you follow my previous advice on creating the right impression. It may not seem appropriate to dress smartly when you are attending the BARB test but that little bit of extra effort in terms of your appearance and bearing will go a long way!

More about the BARB test

Psychometric tests within the British Army are used as a tool to measure the mind and your ability. If we break down the word 'psychometric' we can see that 'psycho' means mind and 'metric' means to measure. BARB is a computer-based, psychometric assessment that was developed by the Defence Evaluation and Research Agency (DERA) and Plymouth University. It is a series of timed questions that assess a candidate's ability to absorb information quickly and logically. The computer automatically calculates the candidate's score, based on the number of correct answers and the time taken. The final score is referred to as the GTI (General Trainability Index). The BARB test has been in use since July 1992.

In order to prepare effectively for BARB test study the following pages, which will provide you with a host of sample test questions. Another great way to help you practise is to purchase your own psychometric testing booklet. These are available from www.how2become.co.uk.

TIPS FOR IMPROVING YOUR BARB TEST SCORES

Once you have completed your BARB test preparation there are still a number of things you can do in order to improve your scores. It is vital that you get a good night's sleep the night before you are due to take the test. There are many reasons for this but the main one is that you will give yourself a better chance of achieving a higher score. This in turn will give you more career options to choose from. It will also ensure that you feel confident before taking the test as fatigue can cause stress, which will inhibit your performance on the day. Make sure that you know exactly where you need to go to take the test. This may sound like an obvious tip but you'll be amazed at how many people get to the test centre late and are then not allowed to sit the BARB. My advice is to go to the test centre a few days before your scheduled date to familiarise yourself fully with the directions and parking facilities etc.

Do not take the test on an empty stomach. You should try to eat a good breakfast on the morning of your test. This doesn't mean eating a great big fry up but instead eating something that is light and that will give you sustained energy throughout the day. A bowl of porridge is great for providing sustained energy or a healthy cereal such as bran flakes with a chopped banana spread over the top.

If your test is scheduled to start at 10am make sure you get there early enough to avoid a last minute panic. It is

far better to get there early and have to hang around rather than get there late and not be able to sit the test at all. Take a small bottle of water with you to keep yourself hydrated and focused. If you wear glasses make sure you take them along with you. You will be using a computer and you need to ensure you can see correctly. The night before the test read any correspondence thoroughly at least twice and make sure you haven't missed anything glaringly obvious. You may be required to take something with you and if you don't do what is required it shows that you are not very good at following instructions – something that is key to a soldier's role. What dress code would you expect and what dress code would you be most impressed with? Remember that you are joining a disciplined service that always looks smart and prepared. Just because you are not a soldier yet, doesn't mean to say you can't start thinking like one. My advice is to go smartly dressed, which will present a good image.

CHAPTER 7
BARB TEST
SAMPLE TEST QUESTIONS

Within this section of the guide I have provided you with a number of sample test questions to help you prepare for the real test. Please note that these are not the exact questions that you will be required to sit on the day. However, they are provided as a useful practice tool in order to help focus your mind on the type of tests you will be sitting. It is also important to point out that during the real test you will be required to answer the questions on a computer screen and how they will be presented will be different to how they are formatted within this guide.

Take a look at the explanations provided and make sure you fully understand what is involved before attempting the practice questions. Once you have completed the practice questions it is important that you take note of where you have gone wrong. Learn from any mistakes as this will help you to further improve your scores during the real test.

Reasoning tests form an integral part of the BARB selection tests within the British Army selection process. These tests are relatively simple to understand once you fully appreciate what is required. The reasoning tests are basically a form of problem solving and you will be asked a number of questions, usually about a relationship between two people. For example, you could be asked a question along the following lines:

Sample question

Richard is taller than Steven. Who is shorter?

The answer in this case would be Steven as the statement suggests that Richard is taller than Steven. Therefore Steven is the shorter of the two.

ANSWER: Steven

Here is another example:

Sample question

Mark is not as wealthy as Jane. Who has less money?

ANSWER: Mark.

The statement suggests that Mark is not as wealthy as Jane therefore suggesting that Jane has more money. Mark therefore has less money and is not as wealthy as Jane.

When you are answering these questions it is important that you READ each question thoroughly. The questions are relatively simple to answer but they can catch you out if you do not understand exactly what the question is asking.

TIPS FOR PASSING THE REASONING TESTS

When you attend the careers office to sit the BARB test you may be asked to take the test on a computer. The computer version of the test will require you to use 'touch screen' answers, which means that instead of using a pen and paper to mark down your answers you will have to touch the computer screen instead. Whilst this is far quicker than writing down your answers, you will need to understand the questions fully before giving your answer.

The question on the screen may appear as follows:

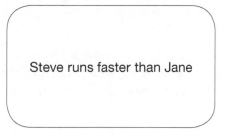

Once you have read the statement you will then need to touch the screen to obtain the question. Make certain that you remember the statement as when you touch the screen it will disappear and you will be given two choices of answer as follows:

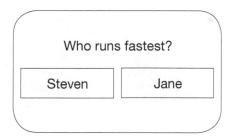

Once the question appears you will then be required to touch the screen in order to indicate your answer. Can you remember what the question was? My tip is to repeat the statement at least three times in your head before touching the screen to obtain the question. Once the question appears you can repeat the statement to yourself that Steven runs faster than Jane and therefore provide yourself with the answer to the question – Steven is the fastest.

Once you fully understand what is required, move on to exercise 1 on the following page. You have 5 minutes in which to answer the 15 questions. Please note that the time limit placed on this exercise will not be the same as the one set during the real BARB test.

Once you have completed the exercise make sure you check thoroughly any questions you got wrong. It is important to do this so that you can improve your scores during the real test

REASONING TEST - EXERCISE 1

Question I
Marcus is not as bright as Andrew. Who is brighter?

Answer

Question 2
Sharon is taller than Sheila. Who is the tallest?

Answer

Question 3
Pauline is stronger than Beverley. Who is the weaker of
the two?

Answer

Question 4
Gary is lighter than Frederick. Who is the heavier?

Answer

Question 5
The black car is faster than the white car. Which car is
the quickest?

Answer

Question 6
Rachel runs faster than her sister Georgia. Who runs
the slowest?

Answer

Question 7
David has more money than Arnold. Who is the poorer?

Answer

Question 8
Jill is weaker than Bill. Who is the strongest?

Answer

Question 9
Hayley sleeps for 10 hours and Julie sleeps for 650 minutes. Who sleeps the longest?

Answer

Question 10
Sadie's shoe size is 7 and Mary's is 9. Who needs the larger size shoes?

Answer

Question 11
George is sadder than Mark. Who is the happier of the two?

Answer

Question 12
Pete is faster than Rick. Who is the slowest?

Answer

Question 13
Jim is older than Brian. Who is the youngest?

Answer

Question 14
Katie eats slower than Lucy. Who is the faster eater?

Answer

Question 15
John finishes the race before Tony. Who ran the slowest?

Answer

Now that you have completed exercise 1, take the time to check over your answers carefully. If you got any of them wrong then make sure you learn from your mistakes. This is a crucial part of your development. Once you are satisfied move on to the next exercise.

ANSWERS TO REASONING TEST - EXERCISE 1

Question 1:   Andrew

Question 2:   Sharon

Question 3:   Beverley

Question 4:   Frederick

Question 5:   The Black Car

Question 6:   Georgia

Question 7:   Arnold

Question 8:   Bill

Question 9:   Julie

Question 10:   Mary

Question 11:   Mark

Question 12:   Rick

Question 13:   Brian

Question 14:   Lucy

Question 15:   Tony

REASONING TEST - EXERCISE 2

Question 1
The red car is twice as fast as the grey car. Which car is slowest?

Answer

Question 2
Julia is half the weight of her neighbour Jonathan. Who is the heaviest?

Answer

Question 3
Barry has been playing darts for three times longer than his team mate Paul. Who has played for the least amount of time?

Answer

Question 4
Jim passed his driving test in 1998 and his wife Gloria passed hers in 1989. Who has held their driving licence the longest?

Answer

Question 5
Darren lives 13 miles away from his place of work. Jessica's workplace is 12 miles away from her home? Who lives the furthest away from their place of work?

Answer

Question 6
Rupert has a motorbike which cost £6,450 and Mark has a

motorbike which cost £5,654. Who has the least expensive motorbike?

Answer

Question 7
Ronald weighs slightly more than Peter. Who is the lightest?

Answer

Question 8
Stuart's house was built in August 1965 and his girlfriend Margaret's house was built in January 1965. Whose house is the oldest?

Answer

Question 9
If Jen has £3.95 and Marcus has 295 pence, who has the least money?

Answer

Question 10
Carol attends the doctor's surgery at 9am and leaves at 9.35am. Harriet attends the doctor's surgery at 9.35am and leaves at 10.09am. Who stayed at the doctors for the least amount of time?

Answer

Question 11
Ben joined the Army on October the 3rd 1997 and left nine years later. Hannah joined the Army on January the 25th 1993 and left on January the 25th 2003. Who stayed in the Army the longest?

Answer [   ]

Question 12
In 2005 a total of 11,400 people joined the Army. In the previous year a total 10,340 joined the Army. In which of the two years did the Army recruit the least amount of people?

Answer [   ]

Question 13
Abdi is wealthier than Maggie. Who is the poorest?

Answer [   ]

Question 14
Stuart rides his bike twice the speed of Simon. Who rides their bike the fastest?

Answer [   ]

Question 15
Michelle takes out a mortgage for £189,500 and Anthony takes out a mortgage for £198,200. Who has the least amount to pay back?

Answer [   ]

Once again, take the time to check over your answers carefully correcting any that you have got wrong before moving onto the next exercise.

ANSWERS TO REASONING TEST - EXERCISE 2

Question 1:   The grey car

Question 2:   Jonathan

Question 3:   Paul

Question 4:   Gloria

Question 5:   Darren

Question 6:   Mark

Question 7:   Peter

Question 8:   Margaret's house

Question 9:   Marcus

Question 10:   Carol

Question 11:   Hannah

Question 12:   2004

Question 13:   Maggie

Question 14:   Stuart

Question 15:   Michelle

REASONING TEST - EXERCISE 3

Question 1
Bill gets 70% of his answers correct during the test whilst Sam got 25% incorrect. Who achieved the highest score in the test?

Answer

Question 2
Richard is not as happy as Graham. Who is the happier?

Answer

Question 3
William has a car that is half as fast as Bill. Who has the slowest car?

Answer

Question 4
Anthony can run twice as fast as Hillary. Who is the slowest runner?

Answer

Question 5
Jean was born in 1971 and Frank was born 3 years later. Who is the eldest?

Answer

Question 6

Peter washed his car for 90 minutes whereas Abdul washed his for 1 hour and twenty minutes. Who washed his car for the longest?

Answer

Question 7

Ahmed is more intelligent than Sinita. Who is the brightest?

Answer

Question 8

Mika passed his motorbike test 18 months ago whereas June passed her motorbike test 350 days ago. Who passed their test first?

Answer

Question 9

Fin carries five bags of shopping home and Dalton carries home seven. Who has the least number of bags to carry?

Answer

Question 10

Naomi arrives at work at 0834 hours and leaves at 1612 hours. Stuart arrives at work at 0915 hours and leaves at 1700 hours. Who stayed at work for the least amount of time?

Answer

Question 11

Preston weighs heavier than Paris. Who is the lightest?

Answer

Question 12
David is not as good as Brian. Who is better?

Answer

Question 13
Ricky is not as fast as Carlos. Who is fastest?

Answer

Question 14
Yasmin is sadder than Beatrice. Who is happier?

Answer

Question 15
Laurence is poorer than Gene. Who is richer?

Answer

Once again, take the time to check over your answers carefully correcting any that you have got wrong before moving onto the next section of the BARB test.

ANSWERS TO REASONING TEST - EXERCISE 3

Question 1:   Sam

Question 2:   Graham

Question 3:   William

Question 4:   Hillary

Question 5:   Jean

Question 6:   Abdul

Question 7:   Ahmed

Question 8:   Mika

Question 9:   Fin

Question 10: Naomi

Question 11: Paris

Question 12: Brian

Question 13: Carlos

Question 14: Beatrice

Question 15: Gene

THE LETTER CHECKING TEST

When you come to sit the BARB test you will be asked to answer questions where you are required to check letters. The aim of this test is to see how fast you can check information that is presented before you. Whilst working in the Army you will be often required to carry out specific tasks which involve the accurate checking of information, equipment and data.

The following is an example of a letter checking question:

Sample question

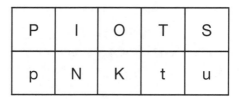

How many letters match?

You can see from the above example that there are columns of letters. In the 1st and 4th box are letters that are identical, albeit one letter is a capital and the other is not. The other boxes contain different letters and therefore do not match. It is your task to identify how many pairs of letters match. In this case I have circled the correct answer for you as being 2 matching pairs.

During the real BARB test you will most probably be asked to sit the computer 'touch-screen' version of the test as opposed to writing down your answers.

When you carry out the test on the computer the question on the screen will be presented to you in a similar format to the following:

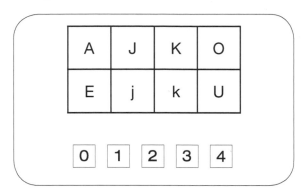

Below the provided letters will be a number of boxes giving you a choice of how many letters match. In this case the answer is 2 as the middle two columns of letters match, whereas the outer two do not. In this case you would touch the number '2' box as your answer. It is important that you work as quickly as possible as the more you score correct, the higher your result will be at the end. As always, deliberate and repetitive practice will serve well to increase your scores.

TIPS FOR IMPROVING YOUR SCORE ON THE LETTER CHECKING TEST

When answering these questions you may find it useful to scan each line downwards in turn and keep a check of how many are correct. When you have scanned the final 4th line you will know how many are correct and then you can touch the number on the screen that corresponds to the right answer.

You will have very little time to answer as many as you can during the real test so you need to work quickly but as accurately as possible. Look out for letters that are similar but not the same, such as:

Q *and* **O**

G *and* **Q**

P *and* **q**

These are the ones that may catch you out so make sure you check carefully.

Now take a look at the first Letter Checking exercise on the following page and see how you get on. There are 15 questions and you have 5 minutes in which to answer them. Simply circle the correct answer with a pen or pencil.

LETTER CHECKING TEST - EXERCISE 1

Question 1

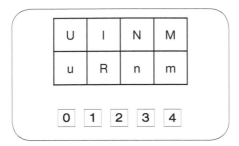

Question 2

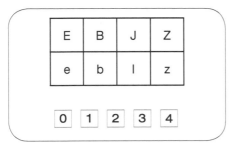

Question 3

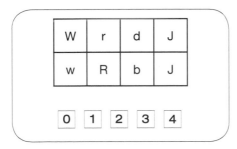

Question 4

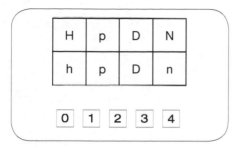

Question 5

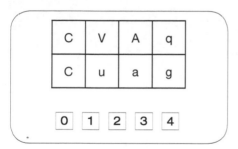

Question 6

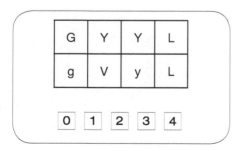

Question 7

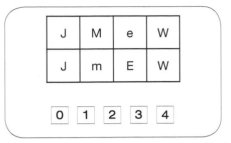

Question 8

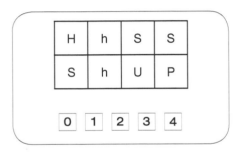

Question 9

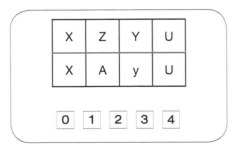

Question 10

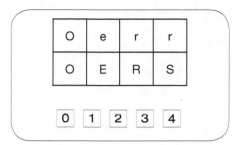

Question 11

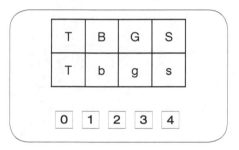

Question 12

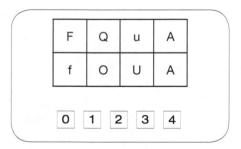

Question 13

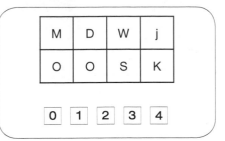

Question 14

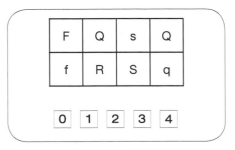

Question 15

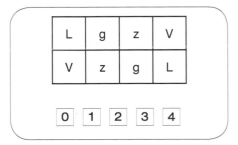

Now that you have completed the first Letter Checking exercise take the time to assess your performance with the answers below. If you got any wrong make sure you return to the question and see where you need to improve.

Once you are satisfied move onto exercise number 2.

ANSWERS TO LETTER CHECKING TEST - EXERCISE 1

Question 1:   3

Question 2:   3

Question 3:   3

Question 4:   4

Question 5:   2

Question 6:   3

Question 7:   4

Question 8:   1

Question 9:   3

Question 10: 3

Question 11: 4

Question 12: 3

Question 13: 0

Question 14: 3

Question 15: 0

LETTER CHECKING TEST - EXERCISE 2

Question 1

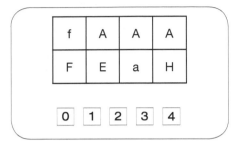

Question 2

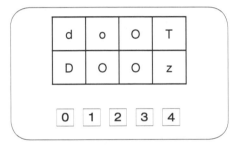

Question 3

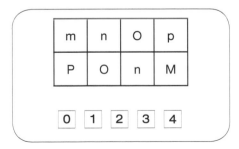

Question 4

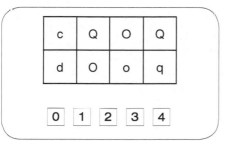

Question 5

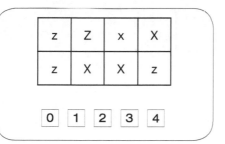

Question 6

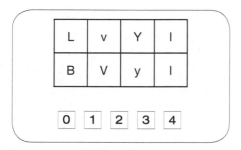

Question 7

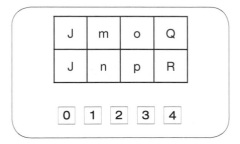

Question 8

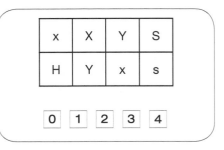

Question 9

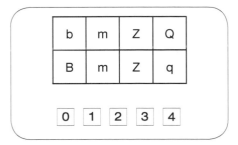

Question 10

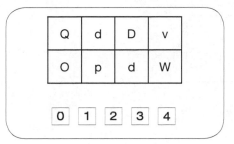

Question 11

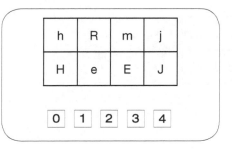

Question 12

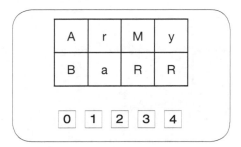

Question 13

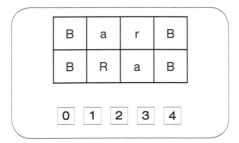

Question 14

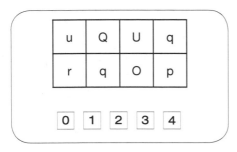

Question 15

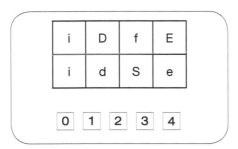

Once again, take the time to assess your performance with the answers below. If you got any wrong make sure you return to the question and see where you need to improve.

Once you are satisfied move onto the next exercise.

ANSWERS TO LETTER CHECKING TEST - EXERCISE 2

Question 1:   2

Question 2:   3

Question 3:   0

Question 4:   2

Question 5:   2

Question 6:   3

Question 7:   1

Question 8:   1

Question 9:   4

Question 10: 1

Question 11: 2

Question 12: 0

Question 13: 2

Question 14: 1

Question 15: 3

LETTER CHECKING TEST - EXERCISE 2

Question 1

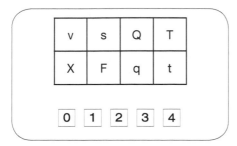

Question 2

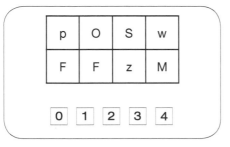

Question 3

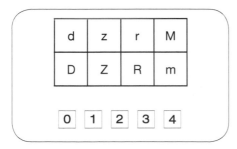

Question 4

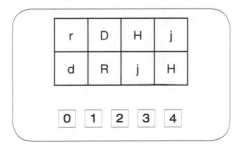

Question 5

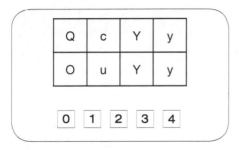

Question 6

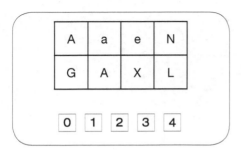

Question 7

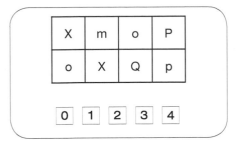

Question 8

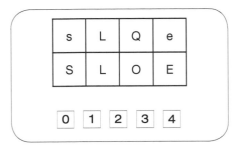

Question 9

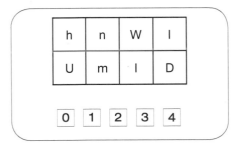

Question 10

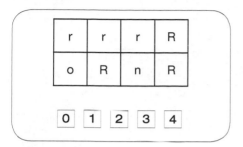

Question 11

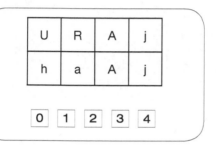

Question 12

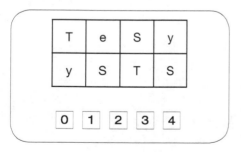

Question 13

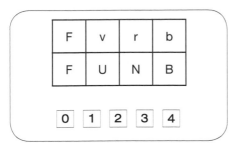

Question 14

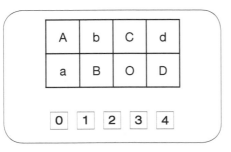

Question 15

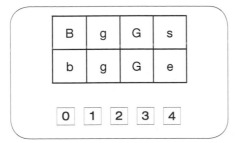

Once again, take the time to assess your performance with the answers below. If you got any wrong make sure you return to the question and see where you need to improve.

Once you are satisfied move onto the next section of the BARB test.

ANSWERS TO LETTER CHECKING TEST - EXERCISE 3

Question 1: 2

Question 2: 0

Question 3: 4

Question 4: 0

Question 5: 2

Question 6: 1

Question 7: 1

Question 8: 3

Question 9: 0

Question 10: 2

Question 11: 2

Question 12: 0

Question 13: 2

Question 14: 3

Question 15: 3

THE DISTANCE NUMBER TEST

During the BARB Test you will have to sit what is called a Distance Number test. This test requires you to analyse three numbers and decide which one of the three fits a certain criteria. For example, you may find 3 numbers appear on your computer screen as follows:

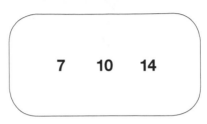

The numbers can appear in any order and will not necessarily increase in value as indicated above. You then have to analyse the numbers and decide which one is the largest number and which one is the smallest.

In this case that would be as follows:

Largest Value = 14

Smallest value = 7

This then leaves you with the number 10. Once you have decided which number remains (in this case the number 10) you then must decide which of the two numbers (7 and 14) is the furthest away from it, hence the title 'Distance Number' test. To work this out you can see that 7 is 3 away from 10 but 14 is 4 away from 10, therefore leaving you with the answer 14.

This may seem complicated at first but with a little practice you will soon grasp the concept of what is required. As with all types of assessment test, the best way to improve your score is to prepare and practise. Try as many practice

questions as possible and you will find that your scores will keep increasing.

On the following pages I have provided you with a number of sample questions for you to prepare. Before you start the test take a look at the following four step approach that will help you to answer the questions.

STEP 1
Out of the three numbers, decide which one is the smallest and which one is the largest.

STEP 2
Then look at the number you are left with.

STEP 3
Now decide which of the two numbers in step 1 is furthest away from the number in step 2

STEP 4
The number that is the furthest away is your answer.

Now move on to exercise 1. There are 30 questions for you to try and you have 15 minutes in which to answer them. The times that are provided in this test are different to times allocated in the real test.

DISTANCE NUMBER TEST - EXERCISE 1

Question 1

```
3      7      9
```

Answer [   ]

Question 2

```
4      8      2
```

Answer [   ]

Question 3

```
1      3      4
```

Answer [   ]

Question 4

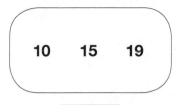

10   15   19

Answer [   ]

Question 5

6   2   9

Answer [   ]

Question 6

7   13   12

Answer [   ]

Question 7

> 67   87   106

Answer [   ]

Question 8

> 2   1   4

Answer [   ]

Question 9

> 12   6   1

Answer [   ]

Question 10

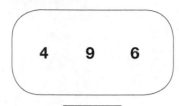

Answer [ ]

Question 11

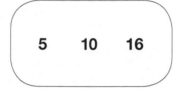

Answer [ ]

Question 12

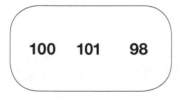

Answer [ ]

Question 13

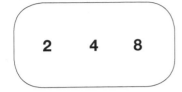

Answer

Question 14

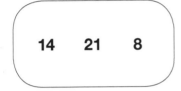

Answer

Question 15

99   108   120

Answer

Question 16

> 7   2   13

Answer [   ]

Question 17

> 14   17   12

Answer [   ]

Question 18

> 9   7   13

Answer [   ]

Question 19

```
11    22    31
```

Answer [   ]

Question 20

```
98    90    80
```

Answer [   ]

Question 21

```
5    3    8
```

Answer [   ]

Question 22

15   4   10

Answer [ ]

Question 23

65   60   72

Answer [ ]

Question 24

45   38   30

Answer [ ]

how2become

Question 25

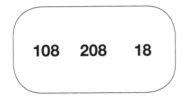

12   8   3

Answer [   ]

Question 26

108   208   18

Answer [   ]

Question 27

7   13   5

Answer [   ]

Question 28

```
  3      8      5
```

Answer [   ]

Question 29

```
 19      6     13
```

Answer [   ]

Question 30

```
  2      9     17
```

Answer [   ]

Now that you have completed the first Distance Number exercise work through your answers checking carefully to see which, if any, you got wrong.

ANSWERS TO DISTANCE NUMBER TEST - EXERCISE 1

Question 1: 3	Question 16: 13
Question 2: 8	Question 17: 17
Question 3: 1	Question 18: 13
Question 4: 10	Question 19: 11
Question 5: 2	Question 20: 80
Question 6: 7	Question 21: 8
Question 7: 67	Question 22: 4
Question 8: 4	Question 23: 72
Question 9: 12	Question 24: 30
Question 10: 9	Question 25: 3
Question 11: 16	Question 26: 208
Question 12: 98	Question 27: 13
Question 13: 8	Question 28: 8
Question 14: 21	Question 29: 6
Question 15: 120	Question 30: 17

Now move on to exercise 2. Again, there are 30 questions for you to try and you have 15 minutes in which to answer them. The times that are provided in this test are different to times allocated in the real test.

DISTANCE NUMBER TEST - EXERCISE 2

Question 1

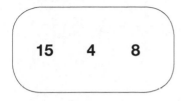

Answer

Question 2

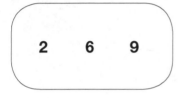

Answer

Question 3

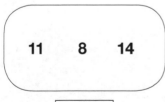

Answer

Question 4

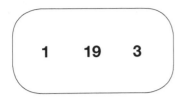

Answer ☐

Question 5

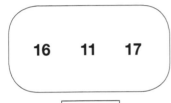

Answer ☐

Question 6

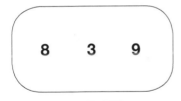

Answer ☐

Question 7

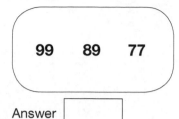

Answer [   ]

Question 8

267   16   134

Answer [   ]

Question 9

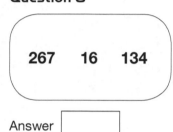

Answer [   ]

Question 10

45   44   42

Answer [   ]

Question 11

15   3   29

Answer [   ]

Question 12

66   14   33

Answer [   ]

Question 13

104   135   167

Answer [   ]

Question 14

474   300   122

Answer [   ]

Question 15

9   8   34

Answer [   ]

Question 16

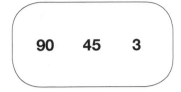

Answer [   ]

Question 17

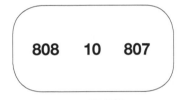

Answer [   ]

Question 18

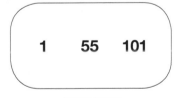

Answer [   ]

Question 19

2   22   44

Answer

Question 20

65   99   128

Answer

Question 21

0   53   105

Answer

Question 22

36   2   17

Answer [   ]

Question 23

1001   501   2

Answer [   ]

Question 24

7   63   6

Answer [   ]

Question 25

809   799   698

Answer [   ]

Question 26

48   25   1

Answer [   ]

Question 27

5   16   25

Answer [   ]

Question 28

788   3   1574

Answer

Question 29

1000   100   599

Answer

Question 30

1971   11   1961

Answer

Now that you have completed Distance Number exercise 2 work through your answers once again checking carefully to see which, if any, you got wrong.

ANSWERS TO DISTANCE NUMBER TEST - EXERCISE 2

Question 1: 15	Question 16: 90
Question 2: 2	Question 17: 10
Question 3: 14	Question 18: 1
Question 4: 19	Question 19: 44
Question 5: 11	Question 20: 65
Question 6: 3	Question 21: 0
Question 7: 77	Question 22: 36
Question 8: 267	Question 23: 1001
Question 9: 2	Question 24: 63
Question 10: 42	Question 25: 698
Question 11: 29	Question 26: 1
Question 12: 66	Question 27: 5
Question 13: 167	Question 28: 1574
Question 14: 122	Question 29: 100
Question 15: 34	Question 30: 11

The Distance Number test, as previously stated, is designed to test your ability to quickly and accurately perform tasks in your head. A good way to practise is to carry out basic addition and subtraction exercises without the use or aid of a calculator. You will find that by just carrying out 10 minute exercises each day you will improve your response times greatly.

On the following pages I have provided you with some numerical reasoning tests to assist you in your preparation. Please note that these tests are not the type that you will come across in the BARB test and they should be used as a practice facility only. There are 30 questions for you to work through and you have 15 minutes in which to complete them. Calculators are not permitted. Simply circle your choice of answer using a pen or pencil.

PRACTICE NUMERACY TEST

Question I

37 + ? = 95

A. 85   B. 45   C. 58   D. 57   E. 122

Question 2

86 - ? = 32

A. 54   B. 45   C. 108   D. 118   E. 68

Question 3

? + 104 = 210

A. 601   B. 314   C. 61   D.106   E.110

Question 4

109 x ? = 218

A. 1   B. 109   C. 12   D. 10   E. 2

Question 5

6 + 9 + 15 = 15 x ?

A. 15   B. 2   C. 3   D. 4   E. 5

Question 6

(34 + 13) − 4 = ? + 3

A. 7   B. 47   C. 51   D. 40   E. 37

Question 7

35 ÷ ? = 10 + 7.5

A. 2   B. 10   C. 4   D. 1   E. 17

Question 8

7 x ? = 28 x 3

A. 2   B. 3   C. 21   D. 15   E. 12

Question 9

100 ÷ 4 = 67 - ?

A. 42   B. 24   C. 57   D. 333   E. 2

Question 10

32 x 9 = 864 ÷ ?

A. 288   B. 3   C. 882   D. 4   E. None of these

Question 11

Following the pattern shown in the number sequence below, what is the missing number?

1   3   9   ?   81   243

A. 18   B. 27   C. 49   D. 21   E. 63

Question 12

If you count from 1 to 100, how many 6s will you pass on the way?

A.10   B. 19   C. 20   D. 11   E. 21

Question 13

50% of 350 equals?

A170   B. 25   C. 175   D. 170   E. 700

Question 14

75% of 1000 equals?

A.   75   B. 0.75   C. 75000   D. 750   E. 7.5

Question 15

40% of 40 equals?

A. 160   B. 4   C. 1600   D. 1.6   E. 16

Question 16

25% of 75 equals?

A. 18   B. 18.75   C. 18.25   D. 25   E. 17.25

Question 17

15% of 500 equals?

A. 75   B. 50   C. 0.75   D. 0.505   E. 750

Question 18

5% of 85 equals?

A. 4   B. 80   C. 4.25   D. 0.85   E. 89.25

Question 19

9876 – 6789 equals?

A. 3078   B. 3085   C. 783   D. 3086   E. 3087

Question 20

27 x 4 equals?

A. 106   B. 107   C. 108   D. 109   E. 110

Question 21

96 ÷ 4 equals?

A. 22   B. 23   C. 24   D. 25   E. 26

Question 22

8765 – 876 equals?

A. 9887   B. 7888   C. 7890   D. 7998   E. 7889

Question 23

623 + 222 equals?

A. 840   B. 845   C. 740   D. 745   E. 940

Question 24

A rectangle has an area of 24cm^2 . The length of one side is 8cm. What is the perimeter of the rectangle?

A. 22 inches   B. 24cm   C. 18cm   D. 22cm   E. 18 inches

Question 25

A square has a perimeter of 36cm. Its area is 81cm². What is the length of one side?

A. 9cm   B. 18cm   C. 9 metres   D. 18 metres   E. 16cm

Question 26

Which of the following is the same as 25/1000?

A. 0.25   B. 0.025   C. 0.0025   D. 40   E. 25000

Question 27

Is 33 divisible by 3?

A. Yes   B. No

Question 28

What is 49% of 1100?

A. 535   B. 536   C. 537   D. 538   E. 539

Question 29

One side of a rectangle is 12cm. If the area of the rectangle is 84cm2, what is the length of the shorter side?

A. 5cm   B. 6cm   C. 7cm   D. 8cm   E. 9cm

Question 30

A rectangle has an area of 8cm2. The length of one side is 2cm. What is the perimeter?

A. 4cm   B. 6cm   C. 8cm   D. 10cm   E. None of these.

Now that you have completed the sample numeracy test work through your answers carefully before moving onto the next section of the BARB test.

ANSWERS TO PRACTICE NUMERACY TEST

Question 1:	C	Question 16:	B
Question 2:	A	Question 17:	A
Question 3:	D	Question 18:	C
Question 4:	E	Question 19:	E
Question 5:	B	Question 20:	C
Question 6:	D	Question 21:	C
Question 7:	A	Question 22:	E
Question 8:	E	Question 23:	B
Question 9:	A	Question 24:	D
Question 10:	B	Question 25:	A
Question 11:	B	Question 26:	B
Question 12:	C	Question 27:	A
Question 13:	C	Question 28:	E
Question 14:	D	Question 29:	C
Question 15:	E	Question 30:	E

SELECTING THE ODD ONE OUT

As part of the BARB test you will be required to sit a selecting the Odd One Out test. The requirement of this test is to simply select the odd one out from a group of words. Take a look at the following sample question:

Sample question

Which of the following is the odd one out?

Ball   Footballer   Tree

The answer to this question is Tree. The reason is that Ball and Footballer are associated together, whereas Tree cannot be placed in the same category as the other two words, so therefore is the odd one out. You may find some words are the opposite of another one, which again is the association or connection. Here's another example.

Sample question

Which of the following is the odd one out?

Warm   Cold   Car

The odd one out in this example is Car. Warm is opposite to Cold, so therefore Car is the odd one out. Now try the exercise on the following page.

Remember to read the questions carefully. When you sit the real test with the Army you may have to take the test on a computer as described in previous pages. An example of a question presented on a computer screen would be as follows:

Sky   Cloud   River

In this particular question River is the odd one out. Allow yourself 2 minutes only to answer as many questions as possible on the following exercise which contains 14 questions. Simply circle which word you believe is the odd one out. Once again the times provided in this sample test are different to the ral test.

SELECTING THE ODD ONE OUT - EXERCISE 1

Question 1

Bark   Sun   Tree

Question 2

Peanut   Mechanic   Spanner

Question 3

Hello   Goodbye   Running

Question 4

Plane   Ship   Centipede

Question 5

Kilo   Gram   Sugar

Question 6

Garage   Swing   Playground

Question 7

Poor   Rich   Grass

Question 8

You   Lady   Me

Question 9

Good   Table   Bad

Question 10

Little   Date   Large

Question 11

Wet   Dry   Ear

Question 12

Old   Young   Light

Question 13

Day   Night   Road

Question 14

Forever   New   Fresh

ANSWERS TO SELECTING THE ODD ONE OUT - EXERCISE 1

Question 1:   Sun

Question 2:   Peanut

Question 3:   Running

Question 4:   Centipede

Question 5:   Sugar

Question 6:   Garage

Question 7:   Grass

Question 8:   Lady

Question 9:   Table

Question 10:   Date

Question 11:   Ear

Question 12:   Light

Question 13:   Road

Question 14:   Forever

Once you have checked all of your answers thoroughly move on to the sample exercise 2 on the following page. In this exercise there are 14 questions and you have 2 minutes in which to complete them.

SELECTING THE ODD ONE OUT - EXERCISE 2

Question I

| Wheel | Art | Painting |

Question 2

| Sunny | Grass | Raining |

Question 3

| Kitchen | Attic | Sea |

Question 4

| **P**ie | Soup | Gravel |

Question 5

| Bike | Farmer | Pigs |

Question 6

Computer   Can   Drink

Question 7

Trousers   Shoes   Belt

Question 8

Men   Women   Army

Question 9

Horrible   Nice   Nasty

Question 10

Window   Glass   Cement

Question II

Spoon   Red   Yellow

Question 12

Money   Car   Bank

Question 13

Cardboard   Queen   Plastic

Question 14

Fix   Wooden   Repair

Once you have completed exercise 2 work through your answers correcting any that you get wrong. Once you have done this simply move on to the next exercise.

ANSWERS TO SELECTING THE ODD ONE OUT - EXERCISE 2

Question 1:   Wheel

Question 2:   Grass

Question 3:   Sea

Question 4:   Gravel

Question 5:   Bike

Question 6:   Computer

Question 7:   Running

Question 8:   Army

Question 9:   Nice

Question 10: Cement

Question 11: Spoon

Question 12: Car

Question 13: Queen

Question 14: Wooden

SELECTING THE ODD ONE OUT - EXERCISE 3

Question 1

Baby   Daylight   Cot

Question 2

Harsh   Firm   Soft

Question 3

Mortar   Sailing   Bricks

Question 4

Dream   Umpire   Cricket

Question 5

Repeat   Laces   Shoes

Question 6

Eat   Dine   Wrist

Question 7

Plate   Brakes   Car

Question 8

Telephone   Communicate   Motorway

Question 9

Reach   Grab   Desire

Question 10

Leaf   Cow   Pony

Question II

Moisturiser   Cream   Distance

Question 12

Road   Battle   Truck

Question 13

Midnight   Moon   Castle

Question 14

Shed   Baking   Food

ANSWERS TO SELECTING THE ODD ONE OUT - EXERCISE 3

Question 1:   Daylight

Question 2:   Soft

Question 3:   Sailing

Question 4:   Dream

Question 5:   Repeat

Question 6:   Wrist

Question 7:   Plate

Question 8:   Motorway

Question 9:   Desire

Question 10:   Leaf

Question 11:   Distance

Question 12:   Battle

Question 13:   Castle

Question 14:   Shed

Once you have checked all of your answers thoroughly move on to the next section of the BARB test which is the symbol rotation test.

SYMBOL ROTATION TEST

During the BARB test you will be required to sit the Symbol Rotation test. The requirement of this test is to identify which symbols are matching by rotation.

Take a look at the following 2 pairs of letters:

You will be able to see that both pairs of letters are the *same*. The only difference is that the letters have each been rotated. Now take a look at the next 2 pairs of letters:

You will see that if each letter on the top row is rotated through all angles, it is impossible to match it up with the bottom letter directly below it. Therefore the letters are said to be a *mirror* image of each other.

During the symbol rotation test you will be required to identify how many pairs of symbols are matching. You will have to rotate the letters/symbols in your mind and decide how many of the pairs that are presented in front of you

actually match. Take a look at the following 3 pairs of letters and decide how many are matching:

Sample question

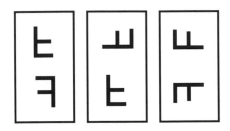

You will see that the letters in the first two boxes can be rotated round to match. The pair in the third box however cannot be rotated to match. Therefore there are <u>two</u> pairs in this sequence that are identical.

Now try the exercise on the following pages. Your task is to identify how many pairs of letters match in each sequence. You have 5 minutes to complete the exercise of 15 questions. Simply circle which answer is correct in the box beneath each question. The times provided in the following sample exercises are not the same as the real test.

SYMBOL ROTATION TEST – EXERCISE 1

Question 1

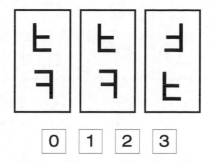

| 0 | 1 | 2 | 3 |

Question 2

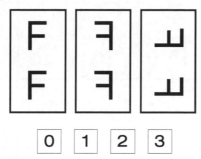

| 0 | 1 | 2 | 3 |

Question 3

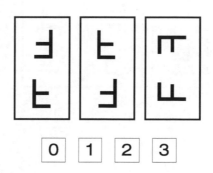

| 0 | 1 | 2 | 3 |

Question 4

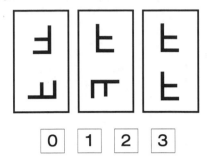

0   1   2   3

Question 5

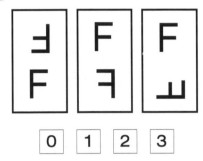

0   1   2   3

Question 6

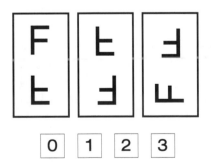

0   1   2   3

Question 7

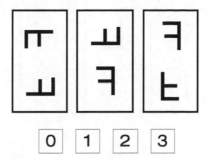

0   1   2   3

Question 8

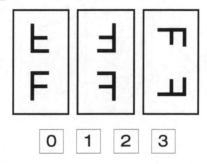

0   1   2   3

Question 9

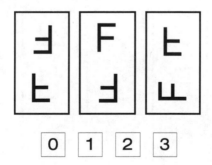

0   1   2   3

Question 10

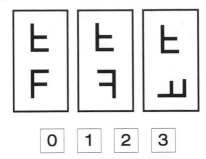

Question 11

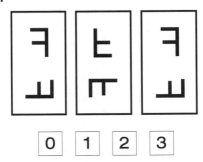

Question 12

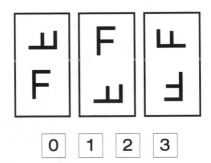

Question 13

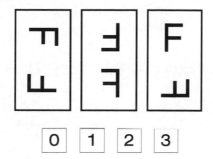

Question 14

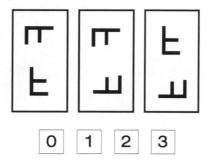

Question 15

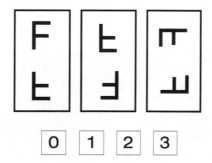

Now that you have completed the exercise take the time to check over your answers carefully before moving on to Symbol Rotation exercise 2.

ANSWERS TO SYMBOL ROTATION TEST - EXERCISE 1

Question 1:   2

Question 2:   3

Question 3:   0

Question 4:   2

Question 5:   1

Question 6:   1

Question 7:   3

Question 8:   0

Question 9:   1

Question 10: 2

Question 11: 3

Question 12: 1

Question 13: 1

Question 14: 3

Question 15: 1

Once again there are 15 questions and you have 5 minutes to work through them. Circle the correct answer in the box provided.

SYMBOL ROTATION TEST – EXERCISE 2

Question I

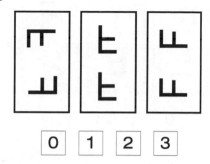

| 0 | 1 | 2 | 3 |

Question 2

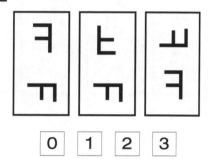

| 0 | 1 | 2 | 3 |

Question 3

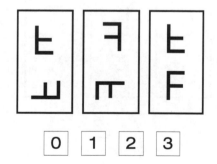

| 0 | 1 | 2 | 3 |

Question 4

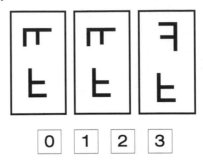

0   1   2   3

Question 5

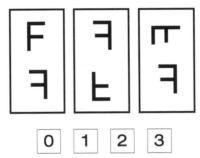

0   1   2   3

Question 6

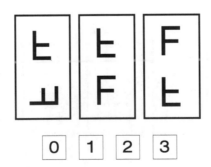

0   1   2   3

Question 7

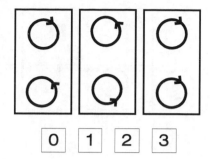

Question 8

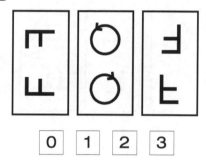

Question 9

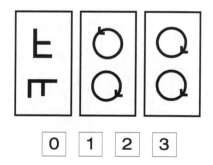

Question 10

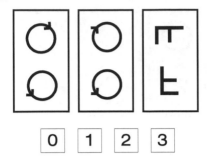

Question 11

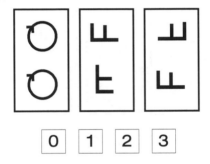

Question 12

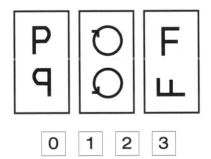

Question 13

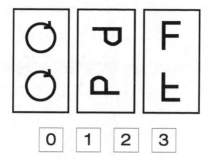

Question 14

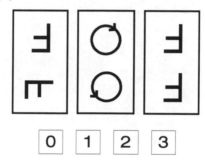

Question 15

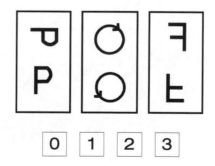

Now that you have completed the exercise take the time to check over your answers carefully before moving onto the next exercise.

ANSWERS TO SYMBOL ROTATION TEST - EXERCISE 2

Question 1:   3

Question 2:   1

Question 3:   2

Question 4:   3

Question 5:   2

Question 6:   1

Question 7:   2

Question 8:   0

Question 9:   2

Question 10: 1

Question 11: 1

Question 12: 1

Question 13: 2

Question 14: 1

Question 15: 2

SYMBOL ROTATION TEST – EXERCISE 3

Question 1

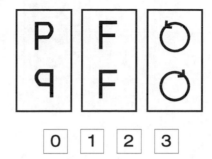

Question 2

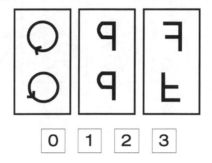

Question 3

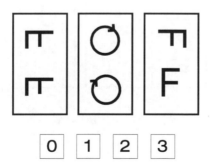

Question 4

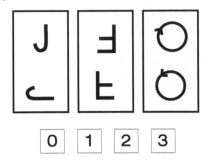

0   1   2   3

Question 5

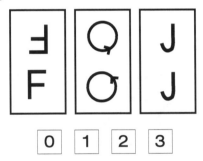

0   1   2   3

Question 6

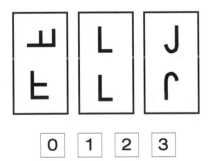

0   1   2   3

Question 7

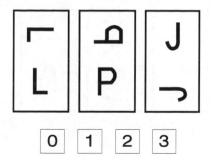

Question 8

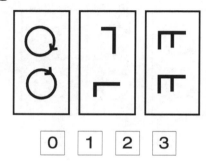

Question 9

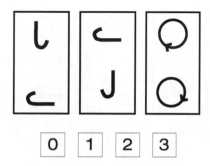

Question 10

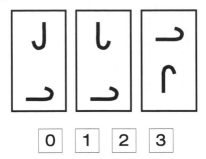

Question 11

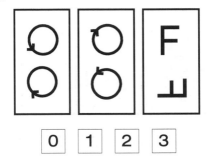

Question 12

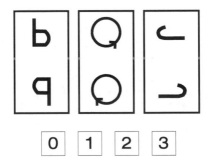

Question 13

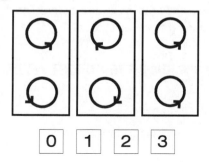

Question 14

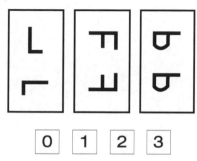

Question 15

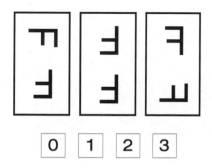

Now that you have completed the exercise take the time to check over your answers carefully before moving on to the final tips for passing the BARB test.

ANSWERS TO SYMBOL ROTATION TEST - EXERCISE 3

Question 1:   1

Question 2:   2

Question 3:   3

Question 4:   1

Question 5:   3

Question 6:   3

Question 7:   2

Question 8:   3

Question 9:   2

Question 10:   1

Question 11:   0

Question 12:   1

Question 13:   3

Question 14:   2

Question 15:   3

FINAL TIPS FOR PASSING THE BARB TEST

Success at the BARB test will be very much dependant on how much, and the type of preparation you carry out. Don't forget to make your preparation deliberate in the essence of carrying out plenty of repetitive practice in the areas that are your most weakest. For example, if you feel that you are poor at the Distance Number test then get yourself of copy of a numerical reasoning test booklet and work hard at the questions contained within it. If you really worried about your testing ability then I would recommend you consider obtaining a personal tutor to assist you. Your practice should be over a prolonged period of time but not by way of cramming the night before your test. Little and often is the key to success.

As previously stated you should take care of what you eat and drink in the build up to the test. Avoid alcohol and caffeine in the few days leading up to the test and get plenty of rest. You will want to be at your best during the test and all of these small areas will help you to improve your scores.

CHAPTER 8
THE ARMY DEVELOPMENT AND SELECTION CENTRE

Within this section of your guide I have provided you with some useful information that will help you to prepare for the Army Development & Selection Centre (ADSC) that forms part of the Parachute Regiment Selection process. The ADSC comes after your initial application and BARB test results and the decision to recommend you for ADSC will rest with your Armed Forces Careers Officer.

The purpose of the ADSC is to assess whether you are suitable for joining the Army but to also see whether the Army is suitable for you. During the two day ADSC you will get to speak to serving recruits and you will have the opportunity to get a feel for life within the Army. Preparation for ADSC should start as soon as you have taken the BARB test and it should be as focused as the previous stages. You will want to be at your best during ADSC and you will want to gain high scores. It is crucial that you give 100% at everything during

the ADSC and that you also create the right impression. The Army will pay for your travel arrangements to attend ADSC and this will usually be by train. You should get to the ADSC in plenty of time. The last thing you should do is arrive late as this will get you off on the wrong foot. I also advise that you attend in a smart formal outfit such as a suit, shirt and tie if you are male and formal outfit if you are female. The majority of candidates will arrive in tracksuits or jeans and trainers. After speaking to serving Army Officer's during the research into this guide it was made perfectly clear that they would prefer to see candidates arrive at ADSC smartly dressed. Make sure your shoes are clean and tidy and remember to take everything with you that is required, including relevant documentation.

ABOUT THE ADSC

There are number of ADSC's across the country where a total of 10,000 people apply in any one year. The two day ADSC is designed to assess whether you are suitable for Army life, whether Army life is suitable for you, and also what jobs you may be suited to if you successfully pass the entire selection process. The entrance level fitness test involves a series of strength tests, fitness tests and a mile-and-a-half run.

THE MEDICAL

One of the very first stages of ADSC is the medical. The medical is a thorough examination that includes various form filling and assessments. You will need to be passed fit by the Army doctor in order to progress to the next stage of the ADSC. If the Army are unsure about a certain aspect of your health then they may refer you to a specialist or doctor for further checks.

THE ICE BREAKER/INITIAL PRESENTATION

During the ADSC you will be required to carry out a two minute 'ice breaker' presentation to the rest of the group. This will normally come following the initial medical. The ice breaker is designed to do exactly what it says – break the ice and the nervousness that is all part of ADSC. You will normally be required to talk about a number of topics relating to yourself such as:

• Name;

• Age;

• Where you are from;

• Who your family consists of;

• Your hobbies and general interests;

• The reasons why you have chosen your regiment/corps;

• Something interesting about you or your most memorable moment;

• Your ambitions in life;

• What you can offer the Army;

• What you are good at and what you are not so good at.

I would advise that you practice carrying out a mini presentation on the above subject areas before you attend the ADSC to your family or a small group of friends. This will help you to reduce any nerves you may have whilst speaking in font of a group of people. When giving your presentation at the ADSC make sure you stand up straight at all times and speak confidently, clearly and concisely. Your ability to communicate with confidence is important and the only way to achieve confidence is through practice. Give your presenta-

tion to everybody in the room instead of looking at just one person. Try to make your presentation interesting and also try to throw in something which is humorous as this will help to break the ice. When speaking about your hobbies and interests make sure you demonstrate that you are an active person who participates in team sports and activities.

Things not to say during your presentation include:

- That you have done little or no preparation for ADSC;
- You don't like being told what to do by others;
- You don't like your job or school;
- You are not very active or physically fit;
- You are not confident of passing ADSC.

GYM TESTS AND THE 1.5 MILE RUN

During the ADSC you will be required to carry out a number of fitness tests in the gym and also a 'best effort' 1.5 mile run. Before you attend the ADSC you should aim to comfortably achieve 50 press ups within two minutes, and 50 sit ups in two minutes. Your 'how to get soldier fit' guide is an excellent resource to help your prepare for both of these. You may not have to carry out a sit up or press up test during the ADSC but you'll certainly be doing lots of them during the evening gym session. I would also recommend you carry out a form of 'step up' exercise. The Chester Step test is a great way to improve your step up performance and this can be obtained through the website www.how2become.co.uk.

During the evening gym session, which will last for approximately 45 minutes, you will be grouped up with other candidates. During a set period of time you will be required

to carry out basic repetitive exercises such as step ups, press ups or sit ups whilst each member of the group runs backwards and forwards between two set points. You will be required to give 100% during these tests so lots of preparation beforehand will work to greatly improve your scores.

As part of the ADSC you will also be required to carry out a 1.5 mile run which should be your best effort. This test always takes place outdoors and it is carried out on an even surface. To begin with, you will carry out a half mile warm up before conducting the actual test. The official army standard requires you to complete the distance in 14 minutes (14 minutes and 30 seconds for juniors). It is very important that you can easily achieve the right minimum standard before you attend the ADSC for a very good reason. It is a well known fact that those applicants who complete the 1.5 mile run in over 14 minutes are far more likely to pick up an injury during training than those applicants who can do the run sub 12 minutes. Therefore it is important that can complete the run in less than 14 minutes before you attend ADSC!

Whilst the minimum standard is 14 minutes, there are varying standards set for the different sections of the Army, depending on which one you are applying for.

THE STRENGTH TESTS

The good thing about the strength tests is that if you are fairly poor at one of them it does not necessarily mean you fail. There are five tests in all that you must complete. Once you have completed the tests your results will be calculated. The Army will also use your height and weight as an assessable factor when determining your strength. If you score poorly on the strength tests then this can mean that you will not be suitable for certain jobs in the Army. An example of this could be building bridges in the Royal Engineers,

First up is pull ups or heaves. You will be required to cling to a bar above your head and attempt to lift yourself up to meet it. I would recommend you be capable of carrying out 10 heaves before you attend ADSC. Whilst this is not essential it will allow you to impress the gym staff and assessors. The tests of back extension, static lift and dynamic lift strength all necessitate standing on pieces of equipment while pulling or pushing weights, and holding it for a set period of time. You will find that a number of these tests are carried out on various machines in the gymnasium. These machines are used to measure your ability to lift weights which are firmly attached to immovable objects. It is the amount of force that you apply to the load cell which is important as this is recorded through a digital reading which is in kilograms of force.

Finally, you will head outside for the jerry can carrying assessment. The objective is to see how far you can one jerry can in each hand without putting them down. Each jerry can will weigh 20kg's.

THE INFORMATION RETENTION TEST

During the ADSC you may be required to sit a form of information retention test. This will be based around an item of military equipment. One of the more common types of test used at the ADSC is the grenade test. The test requires you to listen to a lesson which is based on a specific hand grenade that is used by the Army. During the lesson it is important to listen carefully and absorb the information that is being provided. Once the lesson is complete you will be required to take a test.

Here are some of the more common questions that are used during the test. Important note - the following questions and

answers are samples only and should not be relied upon to be the exact questions you will get asked during your test. The type of grenade used during the test will vary.

Sample question:
What is the name of the grenade?

Sample answer: **L110A1 or L109A1.**

Sample question:
What colour is the grenade?

Sample answer : **L110A1 is Dark blue with white stencilling. L109A1 is deep bronze green.**

Sample question:
What does 'inert' mean?

Sample answer: **The grenade is 'live' but without the explosion.**

Sample question:
What does 'HE' stand for?

Sample answer: **High Explosion'**

Sample question:
What is the range of the grenade?

Sample answer: **20 metres if the enemy is unprotected and 5 metres is the enemy is protected.**

TECHNICAL SELECTION TESTS

The Technical Selection Test (TST) is only for candidates who are applying to join specific branches and trades such as the Royal Engineers, Royal Signals, Royal Electrical and Mechanical Engineers, or the Royal Logistic Corps as an

Ammunition Technician. Some other candidates may also be nominated to take the Technical Selection Test depending on their job choices and qualifications. If the TST applies to you then I would recommend that you spend plenty of time improving your ability to work with numerical information and data prior to attending the ADSC. The type of questions that are normally used during the TST can include interpretation of graphical data, division, subtraction, multiplication, addition, percentages, metric unit conversion, ratios, percentages, fractions, averages, volumes, equations and other similar mathematical calculations. One of the most useful resources to obtain for the Technical Selection Test is a GCSE level maths book.

THE TEAM TASKS

During the ADSC you will be required to carry out a number of team tasks which basically entail moving an item of equipment from A to B.

The priority for you as a candidate is to get involved, work as an effective team member, communicate with your colleagues and provide support and encouragement at every opportunity. It is essential that you get involved as those people who stand in the background hoping that they won't get noticed will fail. At the commencement of the team tasks the ADSC staff will provide you with a brief. Make sure you pay attention and listen to what is required. If you don't listen then you will not be able to complete the task. Try to come up with suitable ideas on how to solve the task. Even if you think your ideas may not work it is far better to participate than to say nothing.

Tips and advice for working effectively as a member of a team during the ADSC

Having the ability to work as part of a team is essential to your career within the Army and you will need to demonstrate this ability during the ADSC. Working as a team does not involve being an individual who is only interested in his or her performance. It is the teams overall performance which should be the focus of attention. There are many different qualities that you'll require in order to become an effective team member.

Working in teams can be very rewarding, but at times it can be difficult and downright frustrating. If there are poor communicators on your team, you may often feel left in the dark, confused or misunderstood. To create a successful team, effective communication methods are necessary for both team members and leaders. For example, during the team tasks that form part of the ADSC you will need to communicate with the other team members when both discussing the task and also whilst providing them with support and encouragement.

In addition to the team tasks there is a strong possibility that you will be asked questions relating to your ability to work as an effective team member during your interview with the ADSO. After all, it is teamwork that makes the Army operate as effectively as it does. Without it, it would not function.

A team's success or failure will be determined by the team's achievements, not your own. Whilst it is good to demonstrate that you can lead a team or show initiative and come up with strong solutions, it is the ability of the team to work together to achieve a goal that will be fundamental to its success. Everybody within a team has a role to play and some people will be better at doing specific tasks than others.

During the ADSC you will be given a set amount of time to discuss how you will carry out a specific task as part of the assessment. This time should be used to work out an effective plan and find out who is good at doing what. During this stage you will need to be vocal and come up with possible solutions to the task that is presented. If you stand in the background and let the others get on with it then you will score poorly. Even if you think your solutions are not very effective I would still advise that you put them forward.

Whatever happens, when working as part of a team be motivated and determined to succeed!

It is also a good idea to shout words of encouragement to other team members during the ADSC team tasks and look out for those people who may be finding it difficult. Offer to help them out and provide them with support if required. Keep remembering that you are part of a team and not an individual whose aim is to solely impress.

When working as a team it is important to listen and respect other people's contributions, even though you may think that they are wrong or your idea is better than theirs. Make sure that everyone is involved when working as part of a team and if you see other people struggling or not contributing then try to involve them in some way.

THE ADSC INTERVIEW

During the ADSC you will be required to sit an interview with the Army Development and Selection Officer (ADSO) that is designed to assess your motivations and suitability for joining the Army. Information relating to this interview including sample questions and responses is contained within an earlier section of this guide.

TIPS FOR PASSING THE ADSC

- Arrive early and wear a formal outfit;

- Make sure you pack everything that you are required to take with you and double check everything;

- Do not put your hands in your pockets at anytime during your stay at the ADSC.

- Do not fold your arms or slouch.

- Make sure you listen very careful to each brief and concentrate at all times. The recruitment staff will ask you questions relating to the information they give you throughout the ADSC.

- During the team tasks ensure you get involved. Do not stay in the background but instead work as part of a team. Encourage others and support each member of your team. If you fail to get involved or work as an effective team member then it is likely that you will fail ADSC.

- Leave all forms of jewellery at home otherwise you'll be required to take it off as soon as you arrive.

- During every assessment and test you must give 100% effort. Even if you are finding it difficult keep going and do not stop.

- Before you attend the ADSC try practising an ice breaker. This effectively means standing up in front of a group of people and introducing yourself.

- Call the Officers 'Sir' or 'Ma'am' or as otherwise directed.

- Even though the ADSO interview is relatively informal, you must still create the right impression. Concentrate on your interview technique, sit up right in the chair, do not slouch and address the selection officer as 'Sir' or 'Ma'am'.

A FEW FINAL WORDS

You have now reached the end of the guide and no doubt you will be ready to start preparing for the Army selection process. Just before you go off and start on your preparation, consider the following.

The majority of candidates who pass the Army selection process have a number of common factors. These are as follows:

1. They believe in themselves.
The first factor is self-belief. Regardless of what anyone tells you, you can pass the selection process and you can achieve high scores. Just like any job of this nature, you have to be prepared to work hard in order to be successful. Make sure you have the self-belief to pass the selection process and fill your mind with positive thoughts.

2. They prepare fully.
The second factor is preparation. Those people who achieve in life prepare fully for every eventuality and that is what you must do when you apply to become a soldier with the British Army. Work very hard and especially concentrate on your weak areas. Within this guide I have spoken about deliberate and repetitive practise. Identify the areas that you are weak on and go all out to improve them.

3. They persevere.
Perseverance is a fantastic word. Everybody comes across obstacles or setbacks in their life, but it is what you do about those setbacks that is important. If you fail at something, then ask yourself 'why' have I failed? This will allow you to improve for next time and if you keep improving and trying, success will eventually follow. Apply this same method of thinking when you apply to become a soldier.

4. They are self-motivated.

How much do you want to join the Army? Do you want it, or do you really want it? When you apply to join the Army you should want it more than anything in the world. Your levels of self motivation will shine through when you walk into the AFCO and when you attend the ADSC. For the weeks and months leading up to the selection process, be motivated as best you can and always keep your fitness levels up as this will serve to increase your levels of motivation.

Work hard, stay focused and be what you want...

Richard McMunn

Richard McMunn

how2become

Visit www.how2become.co.uk to find more titles and courses that will help you to Join the Parachute Regiment, including:

- 1 day intensive training courses

- Online Army BARB testing

- Psychometric testing books

www.how2become.co.uk